Teaching in Further Education

D0768283

You might also like the following FE books from Critical Publishing

The A-Z Guide to Working in Further Education
Jonathan Gravells and Susan Wallace
978-1-909330-85-6

A Complete Guide to the Level 4 Certificate in Education and Training Second edition
Lynn Machin, Duncan Hindmarch, Sandra Murray and Tina Richardson
978-1-910391-09-9

A Complete Guide to the Level 5 Diploma in Education and Training
Lynn Machin, Duncan Hindmarch, Sandra Murray and Tina Richardson
978-1-909682-53-5

Equality and Diversity in Further Education
Sheine Peart
978-1-909330-97-9

Inclusion in Further Education
Lydia Spenceley
978-1-909682-05-4

The Professional Teacher in Further Education
Keith Appleyard and Nancy Appleyard
978-1-909682-01-6

Reflective Teaching and Learning in Further Education
Nancy Appleyard and Keith Appleyard
978-1-909682-86-6

Teaching and Supporting Adult Learners
Jackie Scruton and Belinda Ferguson
978-1-909682-13-9

Understanding the Further Education Sector: A critical guide to policies and practices
Susan Wallace
978-1-909330-21-4

Most of our titles are also available in a range of electronic formats. To order please go to our website www.criticalpublishing.com or contact our distributor, NBN International, 10 Thornbury Road, Plymouth PL6 7PP, telephone 01752 202301 or email orders@nbninternational.com.

Teaching in Further Education

The Inside Story

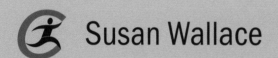 Susan Wallace

FURTHER EDUCATION

First published in 2015 by Critical Publishing Ltd

British Library Cataloguing in Publication Data
A CIP record for this book is available from the British Library

ISBN: 978-1-909682-73-3

This book is also available in the following e-book formats:

MOBI ISBN: 978-1-909682-74-0
EPUB ISBN: 978-1-909682-75-7
Adobe e-book ISBN: 978-1-909682-76-4

Cover and text design by Greensplash Limited
Project Management by Out of House Publishing
Printed and bound in Great Britain by Bell and Bain, Glasgow

Critical Publishing
152 Chester Road
Northwich
CW8 4AL
www.criticalpublishing.com

Contents

Meet the author

Susan Wallace
I am Emeritus Professor of Education at Nottingham Trent University where, for many years, part of my role was to support learning on the initial training courses for teachers in the further education (FE) sector. I taught in the sector myself for ten years, including on BTEC programmes and basic skills provision. My particular interest is in the motivation and behaviour of students in FE, and in mentoring and the ways in which a successful mentoring relationship can support personal and professional development. I have written a range of books, mainly aimed at teachers and student teachers in the sector, and I enjoy hearing readers' own stories of FE, whether it's by email or at speaking engagements and conferences.

Introduction

This is a book of stories. It is also a guidebook and reflective reader on professional practice in further education (FE). These two statements may at first sight appear contradictory. However, a moment's reflection will remind you that the use of stories as a medium for learning is nothing new. We are all familiar with stories that have a purpose, that are designed to develop the reader's understanding and encourage them to think. There is the wisdom set out in Aesop's *Fables*, for example; or classic works such as Bunyan's *A Pilgrim's Progress* or Orwell's *Animal Farm*, written with serious didactic intent to instruct, challenge or enlighten. And of course there are those Victorian morality tales in which misbehaving children meet their doom and terrible consequences follow from the most minor misdemeanours. The stories in this book, however, have more in common with a soap opera and are certainly more down-to-earth, so that anyone who has experience of a FE college will recognise the sort of situations, characters and conflicts portrayed here. And of course, every good story demands its heroes and villains, which is why you'll find some characters who have been to some extent embellished and exaggerated. For example, I hope you would never encounter in real life a manager quite so chilling as the Assistant Principal you'll meet in these pages, or a colleague quite so churlish and unco-operative as the one encountered by our trainee teacher. But these caricatures are present to create and enhance dramatic and interesting situations for you, the reader, to reflect upon and to resolve. And, of course, they are also there to make the story – and the process of learning from it – interesting and, as far as possible, fun.

The story format has been used in order to reproduce the *feel* and *atmosphere* of immersion in a large FE institution. It allows for the exploration of situations which are not usually discussed in conventional textbooks, such as how to cope with intimidating line managers, distracted mentors or learners who complain to you about other teachers. It enables you to consider and seek resolution for common dilemmas, such as being asked to teach an unfamiliar class at short notice, being asked to prioritise teaching over your commitment to professional development or finding yourself in conflict with managers or learners.

Each story here is linked to the next, so that there is also an overarching storyline which runs through the book. This follows the fortunes of three main characters:

*   Matt, who is just starting his teacher training and is picking up some hours of unpaid teaching;

*   Jenni, who has just taken up her first post as a qualified teacher;

*   and Alia, an experienced teacher who is currently undertaking a level 4 Diploma as part of her continuing professional development.

We see how the paths of all three of them cross and re-cross, and how each of them copes with the challenges and dilemmas that arise from their particular roles. Most importantly, at the end of each story there is a set of questions which invite you to reflect on the sometimes complex issues raised; to relate these where appropriate to your own experiences; and to consider what might be learnt in terms of your future practice. Because the problems and challenges presented in the stories are not exclusively about teaching and learning, but reflect day-to-day working in a FE college in its widest sense, the questions focus not only on what takes place in the classroom or workshop. Some of them ask you to consider, for example, issues that relate to the need for professional and appropriate conduct and interaction; co-operation and compromise with colleagues; negotiating relationships with mentors, line managers and senior colleagues; time management; planning; and the weighing of priorities. These sections at each chapter's end, therefore, encourage a 360-degree view of professional practice in that they prompt you to see situations not only from your own perspective but also from the viewpoint of other key players, whether these are learners, colleagues or mentors.

Above all, then, these stories and the questions that follow them are designed to encourage reflection about what constitutes good professional practice, both inside the classroom or workshop, and within the wider institutional context. But why a fictional approach, rather than using *real life* case studies? One answer is that fiction allows us to approach learning in ways which the use of facts does not. In his autobiography, the poet Edwin Muir argues that there are two ways in which stories about our life and our work can be told: either in terms of verifiable data, consisting of dates and documented incidents, or as a *fable,* which doesn't confine itself to facts but which represents more closely the essence or inner *truth* of our experiences. The fable draws upon imagination and can lead us to a clearer understanding of our own unexamined attitudes, assumptions and motives than the bare everyday facts can do. It can prompt a process of reflection on practice which goes beyond the simple analysis of critical incidents and towards a wider exploration of attitudes and expectations. These stories, then, are further education fables, designed to help you reflect on your own role and status – whether you are a new or experienced teacher, or a teacher in training. Engagement with them will help to inform your judgement of how closely your beliefs and practices conform to your own concept of what it means to be a professional educator and trainer in the FE sector.

Stories can have another purpose, too. The American philosopher Richard Rorty argues that empathy and social justice are goals best achieved not through direct, factual enquiry, but through imagination. He suggests, for example, that stories and novels equip us with 'the imaginative ability to see strange people as fellow sufferers' (Rorty, 1989, xvi). By *strange* he doesn't mean *peculiar* (although you may feel that is a fair description of some of the characters you'll meet in these tales!), but *different to us* – whether this is in terms of their age, culture, gender, role or abilities. In other words, stories – which show us the world through someone else's point of view – are one way of enabling us to develop sympathy and empathy; to understand the feelings of others; to put ourselves in their shoes. This is an important attribute for a teacher to develop. Moreover, unlike case studies and accounts of real experience, stories can be shared and discussed with relative safety. No one's real weaknesses are exposed; no one is embarrassed or seen to *fail*.

And yet, on the other hand, apart from a few dramatic exaggerations, these stories are designed to be realistic and relevant enough that they *could* be true – and it is this which makes them useful material for reflection and learning, and for getting a feel of what it's really like to be working in a college of further education in the twenty-first century.

Each story takes a theme – for example, planning a lesson; motivating learners and encouraging appropriate behaviour; working with adult learners; or how to perform well in observations. The stories can be read individually if there is a particular theme you wish to explore, but the real advantage of reading them all consecutively is that you will be able to follow the wider story arc and discover what happens to the characters over time. You will also notice that each chapter is divided into sections. This is simply for ease of reference when addressing the questions at the end of the story. Suggestions for further reading relevant to each story's theme can be found listed at the end of the book.

References

Muir, E (1993) *An Autobiography*. Edinburgh: Canongate Press.

Rorty, R (1989) *Contingency, Irony, and Solidarity*. Cambridge: Cambridge University Press.

Story 1 The best laid plans: planning a lesson

Chapter aims

This story will help you to reflect on:

- how best to set out your lesson content within the framework of a formal lesson plan;

- the importance of the learner activity component to the construction of your plan;

- the question of planning in the wider sense of ensuring, for example, quality provision and adequate teacher support;

- the issues of professionalism which may be encountered by trainee teachers at the very beginning of their teaching career in further education;

- how you may draw on your own vocational or professional background to inform your practice as a teacher in further education;

- the needs of a trainee teacher in terms of support and advice, and how to go about obtaining these.

Part one: Matt makes a plan

Section A

It was difficult enough having to beg this woman for some teaching practice hours. He could have done without her standing so close to him. It didn't help that she was slightly taller than him, so that he had to look up a bit to make eye contact. But he stood his ground. It might look bad if he took a step back. It might look unmannerly, or worse – it might look as though he was easily intimidated. Not exactly the best impression to make when he was trying to sell himself as a teacher.

'You're doing the level 4 Certificate in Education and Training?'

'Yes', he said. 'So I need thirty hours practical teaching. And I was wondering…'

'We can't pay you, you know.' She hadn't cracked a smile yet. Matt wondered now whether he'd made a mistake choosing her as his point of contact. She was Assistant Principal in charge of professional development. Maybe he should have gone in below her – to one of the Curriculum Directors, maybe; or over her head and straight to the top. He'd heard that the Principal was a good bloke with a forces background – someone he could relate to.

'I'm not looking to be paid', he said. 'I just need some teaching hours. I'm volunteering my services, if you like. Thirty hours, to get the Cert. And then I've got my foot on the ladder.'

She was still looking at him as though he was a specimen of something nasty. 'Motor vehicle engineering, did you say?'

'Correct.'

Without breaking eye contact, she put her phone to her ear. It was the latest smartphone. Well, it would be, wouldn't it? And she was standing right by a sign plastered to the corridor wall showing a phone with a big red cross against it. Obviously some regulations didn't apply to Assistant Principals. But did they apply to trainee teachers on teaching practice? This was all going to take some getting used to.

'Paul. It's me.' She turned away to concentrate on her phone conversation and, released from her stare, Matt felt the sort of relief a fish must feel when it gets free of the hook. 'I've got someone here', she said. 'Ex-forces. Wants some teaching hours for the level 4 Cert. The level 4? It's – well, never mind. I'm sending him over to you. Yes, now. Thirty hours. Well, try him. If he can't hack it, let me know. Matt something or other. Right.' She lowered the phone and peered at it just as she had at Matt, as though wondering if there was something wrong with it. 'Okay', she said. 'He'll sort you out. Go over to Motor Vehicle, ask for Paul. He's the section leader. If there's a problem, let me know.' And she was off, away down the corridor, long strides in high heels, like one of those wading birds that stalk the shallows impaling small fish.

Matt walked into the motor vehicle workshop, into the noise and the smell of oil, and it was a bit like coming home. There were several lads in dark blue overalls engaged in various jobs, and a group of them standing in a half circle being briefed by a teacher. The teacher was having to raise his voice over the ambient noise. It all had a familiar feel, apart from the fact that these lads looked about twelve years old.

It turned out they were fourteen. Paul, having set his learners to work, came over and shook hands and started explaining what was what. This class was part of a scheme with local schools, whereby kids could choose to do some of their Key Stage 4 curriculum in college. This wasn't something Matt had reckoned with. Teaching kids? Sounded like a nightmare to him.

'Anyway, I'm ready for a break', said Paul. 'Have you got your DBS clearance?'

'Yes.' Matt had given a copy of his clearance certificate to Assistant Principal Space Invader.

'Take over for a bit, then, yeah? Ten minutes. I'm off for a smoke.'

'Hang about! What are they supposed to be doing? What am I supposed to do with them?'

'Nothing complicated', said Paul, brushing past him. 'Don't worry. They're working on various things. Just keep an eye on them. Make sure they keep on task. Back in ten.' And he was gone.

Nightmare!

Matt took his jacket off and hung it over the back of a chair. He surveyed the workshop. It was a big echoing space and there was a lot of talking and laughter going on, but it was difficult to make out whether this was task-related. So he clasped his hands behind his back, Duke of Edinburgh style, and strolled over to the nearest group, who were lounging around the open bonnet of an old silver Ford Fiesta minus its tyres and propped up on breeze blocks.

'So, what are you up to lads?'

All four of them turned to look at him, and what struck him most forcibly was the complete lack of deference in those looks, the complete lack of manners or desire to please. It wasn't that he expected to see them snapping to attention. He wasn't an NCO any more. But he was – or was going to be – a teacher, and they were learners, and he'd assumed that relationship carried with it some notion of respect. The shock felt physical, like a drink of ice water hitting his stomach.

'Who wants to know?' demanded one of the lads.

'Yeah. Who are you?' chimed in another.

Matt gave them the five-second stare. Then, 'I asked you a question', he said. 'And I expect an answer. What are you working on here?'

This did have some effect. 'Are you an inspector, then?'

'Maybe. And I'm still waiting. You've got – ' Matt looked at his watch, 'ten seconds'.

'We've got to fill in the names of the engine parts', said one of them. He hadn't spoken before. He held out his clipboard for Matt to see. There was a worksheet on it with an outline drawing of the car engine and a list of components below. The learner had drawn in lines to show where a couple of the components were located.

Matt nodded. 'Carry on. You've got ten minutes.' And he strolled over to the next group.

They'd been watching him, and looked a bit wary as he approached. This was better. They had an exhaust system disassembled at their feet.

This time he didn't smile. 'What are you supposed to be doing with this?'

'We don't know', said the smallest lad. He looked barely out of primary school. The cuffs and legs of his overall were folded back in thick rolls and it still swamped him.

'What do you mean, you don't know?'

'We didn't understand what he said.'

'Have you got clipboards? Paper?'

They nodded.

'Well, make a drawing of the assembled parts and label them. You've got ten minutes.'

'But – '

He ignored the protests. He was impressed by his own ability to think on his feet in this unfamiliar setting. But *was* that what they were supposed to be doing? How the hell could he know? It *seemed* a reasonable assumption, based on the task given to the first group. But how was he supposed to keep an eye on the lesson if he had no idea what the plan was? And then, as he approached the third group, another thought struck him. He'd given them ten minutes. What if Paul wasn't back in ten minutes?What were they supposed to be doing next? What could he do with them? Well, he could wing it. He could talk them through internal combustion. Or he could demonstrate some standard procedure or other. But how would he know whether they'd covered this already? How would he know whether it was even part of their curriculum? If he wasted time covering some topic he wasn't supposed to, that would probably be his thirty hours teaching down the toilet. And then he'd be well and truly –

The double doors creaked and slammed. Paul was back. He walked over and stood by Matt, smelling of fags. 'Alright?' He looked around at the groups of lads, engaged on their various tasks. 'Looks like you've managed them ok.'

'Well–'

'So when do you want to start these thirty hours, then?'

'Listen, mate', said Matt, 'I appreciate it. But if I'm going to do anything with them I'm going to need to see a plan.'

'A plan?'

'A plan, yeah. You know, what they're supposed to be doing each lesson and how long they get to do it. And how you assess them on it. All that kind of stuff.'

'Oh right. You have to do that sort of thing, do you? For your qualification? To be honest, I only do those when I have to, when I'm being observed. I've been in this game years. I don't need to write out a plan for every lesson. I mean, come on. If you need to show you've got a plan, obviously you'll have to write it. You wouldn't expect me to do it for you.'

'Well hang on a minute. They're your learners. I'm not being paid to teach them. So technic-ally, I'd be teaching thirty hours' worth of your lessons. As far as I can see, that means you'll need to at least tell me what I should be covering. Surely?'

'Yeah, fine, I can do that.' It sounded as though Paul felt even this was asking a lot.

'Okay,' said Matt. 'Thanks. So can you just show me what a plan would look like?'

'A lesson plan? Nah, I don't think I've kept any. Last inspection was a couple of years ago. But there's probably some sort of pro-forma on the intranet.'

'Okay. Great. How do I get on the intranet?'

'You need a password. Erm, but now I think about it, you don't get access unless you're actually employed here.'

'Okay. Listen, mate, I need to think this over. Just tell me one thing: out of interest, what was that group over there supposed to be doing with the exhaust system?'

Paul looked over at the lads, heads bent now over their clipboards. 'To be honest,' he said, 'I can't remember. But whatever it was, they're getting on with it.'

Section B

The only sensible option, Matt decided, was to go back to Ms Space Invader and re-negotiate. This time she saw him in her office, which was a relief because now at least there was a desk separating them. As it turned out, he was only in there a couple of minutes, during which she didn't do the sinister eyeballing thing either. She was too busy glancing at her watch, her phone and her computer screen, obviously impatient to get shot of him and get back to whatever it was she had been doing.

'No lesson plans?' she said. 'That's interesting.' And she frowned briefly, appearing to be filing that fact away for later.

'So I wondered whether -'

'How's your literacy?'

'Good,' said Matt.

'I'll put you with Alia, then,' she said, fishing out her phone. 'She'll find you some hours on adult literacy. She's a good role model for lesson planning. She'll be in the Literacy Centre now. I'll call her and let her know you're on your way.'

'But – thanks – but just a minute. Hang on. I'm not planning to teach *literacy*. I mean, long term, it's not my -'

'Teaching practice is teaching practice', she intoned, 'for your immediate purposes, anyway. Get used to a bit of lesson planning with Alia, and then you can apply it to whatever subject you're teaching.'

'But–'

'Thirty hours on literacy. Best I can do. Take it or leave it.'

Matt took it.

Over in the Literacy Centre he introduced himself and got the impression that Alia was not overkeen about taking him on. But she was pleasant enough, and invited him to sit at the back and observe the rest of the lesson that she was currently teaching. There were thirteen learners, all adults. Matt estimated the age range to be from about twenty-five to around sixty. They were sitting along three sides of an open square. Alia was at the open end, and on the wall behind her was a screen on which she had been in the process of showing a PowerPoint presentation. Before she resumed she made a brief introduction:

'Everyone, this is Matt. He's come to see what we're doing today. If he likes what he sees, he'll be coming along to work with us occasionally over the next few weeks.'

One or two of the learners said hello to him, and several of them turned in their seats and smiled at him. Matt smiled and nodded back. As introductions went, that was a pretty good one. It didn't draw attention to his lack of experience. It didn't make it sound as though she was doing him a favour. In fact, this was someone Matt felt he could work with. So he leaned back, folded his arms and settled down to watch.

Section C

Later, over coffee in the college refectory, they put together an operational plan. Alia made it a condition of his involvement that he should first observe her teaching five sessions with the class he would be working with before he embarked on teaching them himself. The first two hours of his teaching should be done jointly with her, using a team teaching approach. If she was satisfied that he was up to it, he would teach the remaining hours solo, but always with Alia in the room as observer. This made complete sense. However scary the prospect of teaching literacy was, it was reassuring to be working within clear and logical parameters. He told her so.

'What did you think you'd be teaching?' she asked him.

'Something I know something about.'

'Bit much to ask at this place. But really, what?'

'Motor vehicle engineering,' he said. 'I can do that with my eyes shut. Literally. With my eyes shut. But I can't teach it without a plan.'

'No-one can teach without a plan,' she said. 'And if anybody says they can, don't listen. You're doing the Certificate? That means we're in the same boat. I'm doing the Diploma. So we're both trainees together. Both polishing our lesson plans. Come on, cheer up. You look worried.'

'Never seen myself as a literacy teacher', said Matt. 'That's all.'

'Well, when you've observed a few sessions and you've seen what it's all about, you can make an informed decision, can't you? If you decide it's not for you, that's fine.'

Easy for her to say. He needed his hours. He would teach bloody flower arranging if he had to.

Section D

The first two one-hour sessions he just sat at the back, watching and taking notes, with Alia's lesson plan in front of him. Her plans were set out in grid format which allowed him to follow the sequence of activities as they unfolded. They included a column for teacher activity and one for learner activity, and Matt was interested to see that there was more going on in the second column than in the first. 'Well, of course', Alia said to him, when he questioned her about this after his first hour of observing. 'This process is about them learning. They're the key players here. I could teach and talk until the cows come home, but that doesn't necessarily mean they're learning anything. And that's also why there needs to be that assessment column in there, see?' It made complete sense to him. He began to think he had fallen on his feet here.

On the third lesson he got drawn in without really noticing what was happening, until he found himself working one-to-one with the learner called Ralph, a big untidy bloke of about 50, who had been turning round repeatedly to ask advice. They were working on the use of *a* and *an*. Alia had put a list of words and phrases up on the whiteboard and asked the class to write down each word with the correct indefinite article. Ralph was having trouble. Matt scraped his chair over to sit next to him. 'I'll tell you what mate', he said, 'try saying them out loud.'

This worked quite well, Ralph writing slowly but clearly in a forward sloping script: *a nice cup of tea; an egg; a bird...* Matt's concentration drifted for a minute as he watched Alia laughing with two of the women learners at the other side of the room. When he looked back at Ralph's work he saw that he had added to his list: *an horse* and *an hat.*

'Whoa, hang on, Ralph. What's this, mate?'

'What?' Ralph sounded anxious. 'This? It's a norse and a nat. That's right, innit?'

'Ah! Right. No. Well, I can see what you're doing there. Yeah. That's how you *say* them, Ralph, right? Because round here you don't sound the H, do you, you 'orrible lot.'

Ralph looked at him with alarm. 'What?'

Matt got the feeling he wasn't handling this very well, so he signalled at Alia to rescue him.

Afterwards they talked this over.

'It was good you picked that up', Alia said. 'I should have factored that into the lesson plan: a bit about local pronunciation. And something about posh folks saying "an hotel".'

'Do they?'

'Apparently so. I don't know any myself.'

Matt smiled. 'I scared him though. And I thought I was being friendly.'

'It'll come right', said Alia, 'Remember, some of these learners have had bad experiences with teachers. Their confidence has been undermined by criticism. They're vulnerable. More vulnerable than they look.'

Section E

Before they packed up to leave, she suggested that Matt should revise her lesson plan by putting something in about pronunciation. That evening he set about the task. Opening up the electronic version she had emailed him, he inserted a new row into the grid and filled in the *learning outcome* box. Then he considered the other columns. So far, the new row looked like this:

Outcome	Teacher activity	Learner activity	Assessment	Resources	Differentiation
Outcome: Demonstrate correct use of a/an (Topic: Pronunciation and use of a/an)					

Now, obviously the teacher was going to have to do some explaining first, about the necessity of going by the spelling when deciding between *a* and *an*, rather than by local pronunciation or accent. And there would need to be examples to make this point clear. So it would look like this:

Topic/outcome	Teacher activity	Learner activity	Assessment	Resources	Differentiation
Outcome: Demonstrate correct use of a/an (Topic: Pronunciation and use of a/an)	Explain that a/an depends on whether a word begins with a consonant or vowel, not on how it's pronounced locally. Give examples: *horse* and *hat*.				

Okay. So then the learner activity had to do two things: it had to provide them with practice in order to consolidate what had been learnt and it had to allow the teacher to check that each learner had understood. So the obvious thing would be to have the learners tackle a list of words, some beginning with H and some beginning with a vowel, and decide whether each took *a* or *an*. When he had put that in, the plan looked like this:

Topic/ outcome	Teacher activity	Learner activity	Assessment	Resources	Differentiation
Outcome: Demonstrate correct use of a/an (Topic: Pronunciation and use of a/an)	Explain that a/an depends on whether a word begins with a consonant or vowel, not on how it's pronounced locally. Give examples: *horse* and *hat.*	Choose correct article for a list of words beginning with H or a vowel. Write down correctly. Do first two as a class with the teacher to build confidence.			

Matt was pleased with that bit about building confidence. Now the next two columns were easy. The teacher could assess whether learners were achieving the learning outcome by having a look to see whether the work they were producing under *Learner activity* was done correctly. This would involve walking around the classroom, observing the work in progress. And the resources? Well, plenty of choice here. The list of words could be put up on a whiteboard or displayed via data projector or printed out as individual hard copy handouts. He would probably go for the whiteboard as being the most efficient and reliable way of doing it. So that was the row almost finished:

Topic/ outcome	Teacher activity	Learner activity	Assessment	Resources	Differentiation
Outcome: Demonstrate correct use of a/an (Topic: Pronunciation and use of a/an)	Explain that a/an depends on whether a word begins with a consonant or vowel, not on how it's pronounced locally. Give examples: *horse* and *hat.*	Choose correct article for a list of words beginning with H or a vowel. Write down correctly. Do first two as a class with the teacher to build confidence.	Teacher observes work in progress and gives formative feedback.	Whiteboard and pens.	

He was quite pleased with the bit about *formative feedback*, too. It was something Alia had explained to him after the second time he'd watched her teach. He'd written down what she said at the time. Formative feedback: *Feedback that guides the learner towards improving their performance, rather than simply telling them whether it's correct, incorrect, good, bad or indifferent.* Good one. But what about the final column – the one about differentiation? What was he going to put in there? After a bit of thought, he added a sentence or two. Kept it general. That would have to do. He attached it to an email and sent it to Alia before he over-thought it.

Topic/ outcome	Teacher activity	Learner activity	Assessment	Resources	Differentiation
Outcome: Demonstrate correct use of a/an (Topic: Pronunciation and use of a/an)	Explain that a/ an depends on whether a word begins with a consonant or vowel, not on how it's pronounced locally. Give examples: *horse* and *hat*.	Choose correct article for a list of words beginning with H or a vowel. Write down correctly. Do first two as a class with the teacher to build confidence.	Teacher observes work in progress and gives formative feedback.	Whiteboard and pens.	An extra list of words for learners who need more practice. An extension activity for learners who have already achieved the outcome.

Section F

When they met for him to observe the next lesson Alia congratulated him on the plan. Matt felt well pleased with himself, and was just heading for his usual seat at the back and another hour of watching and listening when she called him back.

'Put your list of words up on the whiteboard, then', she said. 'Let's see how it works in practice.'

'Me?'

'Of course you. Come on. We've got about three minutes before we start. And then – how long do you estimate this bit'll take?'

Matt thought, at a rough guess, about fifteen minutes.

And he was pretty much spot on. After the first minute or so, looking at that horseshoe of friendly faces, and with Alia smiling and nodding from his old seat at the back, his nervous-ness evaporated and he was into his stride. The plan worked. The learners seemed to enjoy themselves, and he certainly did. When he sat back down after a quarter of an hour it was with some reluctance. And at the end of the lesson, when the learners had all packed up their stuff and gone, he was still feeling the buzz.

'So what do you reckon, then?' said Alia, looking up from the briefcase she was packing and smiling at him.

'Me or you?'

'You.'

'Yeah, good', he said. 'It worked. It was good.'

'Anything you'd do differently?' she asked. And then she must have seen his face fall because she added quickly, 'I'm not saying it wasn't good. I just want you to get into the habit of evaluating. You know, what worked well, and why. What could have worked better. Was the learning outcome achieved…'

'But that's not the same as assessment?'

'No. Assessment is about individual learner achievement. Evaluation is about how well your lesson has worked in every respect, including timing, classroom behaviour, everything. Okay? Got to dash, Matt. Sorry. I've got another class. Have a great weekend and I'll see you Monday.'

It wasn't until she'd gone that Matt noticed the bulging brown A4 envelope under the table at the back of the room. It must have fallen out of someone's bag. Had it been there when they all came in? If so, he hadn't noticed it. The previous group in here had been the foundation degree class. They'd been piling out in a hurry after keeping Alia's class waiting to get in. He got down on all fours and fished the envelope out. It wasn't suspiciously heavy and it wasn't suspiciously light. Gingerly he opened the flap and looked inside.

Whatever he expected to find, it wasn't this. Packed in two bundles was what must have been at least a grand in ten pound notes.

Part two: Critical thinking activities

Some of the tasks which follow require you to reflect on details of the story you've just read and to make professional judgements about incidents and conversations in terms of what is acceptable or desirable professional practice and what is not. These tasks also encourage you to consider how such situations might relate to, or arise in, your own experience as a teacher. Other tasks suggest practical exercises aimed at helping you to consolidate what you have learnt. In carrying out both these types of tasks you may find it useful to keep a reflective journal, or to engage in discussion with a colleague or mentor, or – even better – both.

Activity 1

In section A of the story we see Matt requesting the teaching hours he needs in order to complete his initial teaching qualification. The request is quickly granted, so we could say that this initial meeting is a successful one for Matt. However, you may find it useful to consider the following questions:

a) What sort of questions might it have been wise for Matt to ask at this point?

b) Why do you think he didn't ask them?

c) How would you rate the senior manager's handling of this meeting?

d) What might she have done differently?

e) Have you ever found yourself in a similar situation, asking (or being asked) for teaching practice hours? If so, how did that experience compare with Matt's?

f) What are the wider issues about planning that this encounter raises?

Activity 2

In the second part of section A, Matt meets Paul and his class. There's a lot going on in this workshop encounter. The following questions will help to unpick the main points.

a) How would you rate Paul's professionalism as a teacher and colleague? Consider this question both in his interactions with Matt and in his classroom practices.

b) List four things that you, if you were in Paul's place, would have done differently.

c) In your view, how well does Matt handle the situation?

d) List two things you would congratulate him on, and two things you would suggest he could have done differently.

e) Identify two instances in which he was able to draw on his vocational and professional background to help him in this situation.

f) Think back to your first experience of stepping into a further education classroom as a teacher. How did it compare to Matt's? What elements of your own previous vocational experience were you able to draw on, if any?

g) Look again at the exhaust system task which Matt set, off the top of his head, for the second group of learners. Now, using his later line of lesson planning as a template (section E), plan out that task under the same headings. How does it look? In filling in the *Outcome* column you will have had to deduce, from the learner activity he set, what outcome he had in mind. In a good lesson plan this will almost always be possible to do, because in order to assess whether the outcome has been achieved, the teacher must ensure learners have an opportunity to demonstrate what they can do. For this reason, the three key columns – outcome, learner activity, and assessment – will always echo one another, like this:

» outcome – *what the learners will be able to do;*

» learner activity – *an opportunity for the learners to practice and demonstrate whether they can do it;*

» assessment – *opportunities for the teacher to judge whether the outcome is achieved.*

If your mini-plan doesn't do this, have another look at it.

Activity 3

In section B, Matt returns to the Assistant Principal to renegotiate his placement.

a) In your view, was this the best way forward? Would you have done the same in his position? Have you ever been in a similar teaching practice situation where you felt inadequately supported? What action did you take, if any?

b) Matt tells the Assistant Principal about Paul's lack of a lesson plan. Was he right to do this, in your view? Was there an alternative way he could have handled this?

c) He finds himself hustled into an unfamiliar subject area. Have you, or anyone you know, had a similar experience? What was your initial reaction when you read of this happening to Matt? What do you think might be some of the advantages and disadvantages for Matt of being moved out of his comfort zone like this?

d) Can you identify any issues that this section of the story raises about *planning* in the wider sense?

Activity 4

In section C, Matt meets Alia, and we get the impression that he might at last be in a safe pair of hands.

a) List four clues this section gives us that Alia is going to prove to be a good mentor and role model.

b) Look carefully at the schedule she and Matt devise for him. How would you rate this as a piece of *planning*? What are its advantages (i) for Matt and (ii) for Alia?

c) Think about your own induction to teaching. What sort of a plan did it follow? Did you have any say in the drawing up of the plan? If there was no clear plan, or there was one which didn't really work well for you, what would have been your ideal plan? How would it compare with the one Alia and Matt devised?

Activity 5

In section D, we see Matt observing and beginning to involve himself in the teaching.

a) Matt reflects on the proportion of learner activity to teacher activity in Alia's lesson plans. What is the wider point that he is beginning to understand here? How does an emphasis on the learners' activities help with lesson planning?

b) When Matt is drawn in to try and help Ralph, he gets some things right and some things wrong. What would you say were his strengths as a teacher at this very early stage of his career; and what areas does he need to work on?

c) Think about how Alia responds to him at this point. How would you rate her as a mentor? How does her approach compare with that of the mentoring you have received, or have provided?

Activity 6

We discover in section E that Alia has suggested Matt sets out the additional lesson content he's come up with as part of the formal lesson plan.

a) If asked to do the same, is there anything about the planning that you would have done differently? If so, think about your reasons for this. How would you explain your reasons to, for example, a colleague or mentor?

b) Think about a lesson or part of a lesson which you will be teaching in the near future. It may be for a whole group or for individual one-to-one support. Now, using the same pro forma as Matt, set out your plan formally under the same headings he has used. Note down any insights this gives you into the teaching/learning process.

c) Are there additional headings which would be useful for your purposes? For example, would you find it helpful to have a column indicating the time or duration of each component or activity?

Activity 7

Later, in section F, we see Matt being encouraged to evaluate the part of the lesson that he has planned.

a) How would you explain, in your own words, the difference between *assessment* and *evaluation*?

b) Because our evaluation of a lesson is useful in planning the next one, you may find it helpful to incorporate an additional column into the lesson plan you produced for activity 6, and head it: *Evaluation*. This will allow you to add brief comments immediately after the lesson while all is fresh in your mind, about what worked well, what didn't, how well you'd estimated the time needed for each component, and so on.

And finally...

» *You will find some helpful texts relating to the topics covered in this story listed under Further Reading at the back of this book.*

» *To find out more about the envelope of cash and discover what happened next, you'll need to read on...*

Story 2   Assessing learner needs and assessing learning

Chapter aims

This story will help you to reflect on:

- the different purposes for which assessment may be used;

- the distinction between assessing learner needs and assessing learner attainment;

- the importance of diagnostic assessment;

- the purpose and practice of differentiation by outcome;

- the purposes of formative and summative assessment;

- the meaning and application of the terms *validity* and *reliability*;

- the importance of providing learners with clear and constructive feedback;

- the needs of a newly qualified teacher in terms of support and advice, and how to go about obtaining these.

Part one: Jenni and the question of assessment

Section A

Monday

When we did our teacher training last year we had to keep a reflective journal as part of our assessed work and the tutors were always telling us that, whatever stage of your teaching career you're at, it's always useful to keep a journal for noting down insights and critical incidents and good ideas and ideas that didn't work so well. So here I am, soon after the beginning of my first term as a full-time qualified teacher in FE, following their advice. Last week – the first week of term – there just wasn't any time to write anything. Chaos!

Just finding my way around the various buildings was a challenge. And trying to remember people's names, and getting to grips with the online registers, and sorting out a pass for the car park that actually works. I'm supposed to have a mentor for this first year, but I haven't been able to track one down yet. So I just ask advice from anybody I can get hold of. They all seem okay in this department, the ones I've met, anyway. Now I'm into my second week I've got two problems that are weighing on my mind, so hopefully writing about them will help me think them through. The first is my level 2 group where most of the learners seem to have trouble grasping even the most basic information. Well actually – if I'm honest – part of the trouble may be that they don't shut up for long enough to actually hear anything I'm saying to them. And my second problem is that I've apparently been allocated a trainee teacher to come and observe me and – guess what – it's that level 2 class he's going to watch me teaching! Nightmare!

So I've got to get on top of this. What happened today was fairly typical of how it's been with that group so far. I walk in and there's only about half of them there. While we're waiting for the rest to arrive I use the time to go around and talk to individual learners, try to get to know a bit about them. It's one way of informally assessing their learning needs. I found out, for example, that at least one of them, Zaneb, didn't apply for this course and only ended up on it because she didn't get the GCSE grades she needed. That could explain her can't-be-bothered-to-listen attitude. And there may be others in the same position. Anyway, when I had a full class I got started with a recap from the previous lesson. I tried doing it by asking them questions, but had to give up on that because I just wasn't getting any answers. So I did the recap myself and then went on to the new stuff, using PowerPoint. I'd tried to make the slides interesting, with animations and web-links. But the learners just slumped there, some of them not even looking at the screen but just talking among themselves. Those who did pay some attention took no notes. There was no response when I asked questions. Gradually the talking rose in volume so that I was having to raise my voice to make myself heard over it. When I'd finished showing the slides I found that my planned question and answer session got no response at all, so I decided to assess what they'd learnt by giving them a written quiz. Disaster. No one got more than five out of ten, and some of them wrote down no answers at all. (Was this because they didn't know them, or because they couldn't be bothered?)

And now I've got this guy, Matt, coming in to watch me tomorrow, supposedly to see how it's done. I think the only thing I can do is to be honest with him, tell him the problems I'm encountering, tell him what solutions I'm planning to try, and discuss with him at the end how he thinks it went. But what are these solutions going to be?

I think the first one has to be to plan activities that provide opportunities for some *diagnostic assessment*. I need to find out what these learners already know and what they don't, because if I'm not clear where they're starting from in terms of their current knowledge and understanding, how am I going to be able to get them to where they need to be? And I also need to plan for the probability that they're not all starting from the same place. Some will already be ahead of others. So that means my lesson plans in future need to incorporate differentiated tasks and activities. If each learner is able to get something out of the lesson at a level appropriate to their current ability and understanding there'll hopefully be fewer glazed looks and failures to engage.

Section B

Tuesday

Well, at least Matt the student teacher seems a really nice guy. He's quite a bit older than me, I think, which worried me at first because he's supposed to be learning from me. A bit like teaching learners who are older than you – always a scary idea. But he was obviously cool with it, and I forgot about the age difference after a bit. It seemed to make a difference just having him in there. The group was quieter and obviously a bit suspicious about what he was there for. He doesn't look like a student teacher. He looks more as though he's in charge – although he just sat at the back and watched and didn't say anything. But he looked relaxed and comfortable about being there, and it was very interesting the way this clearly made the learners view him as someone in authority rather than as an easy target. I think there's probably something I can learn from this.

Anyway, the lesson went okay this time, thank goodness. The change of approach seemed to work much better. Basically, my lesson plan consisted of three group activities that gave the learners an opportunity to demonstrate whatever skills and knowledge they've already got. Each activity was presented like a game. In the first one each group (and they chose their own groups for this one) had to pretend they were running a business and come up with an idea that would sell – a bit like *The Apprentice*. Wandering around and watching them, I was able to identify learners who, for whatever reason, weren't joining in or pulling their weight. Then for the second activity – a true/false quiz on the basics of this whole vocational area – I reorganised the groups so that those disengaged learners were all grouped together. That gave me a better chance to assess individually whether they lacked the basic knowledge or just weren't interested. For the third activity I got the groups to swap around again and asked them to devise a set of questions to test the knowledge of the other groups. This showed up some interesting gaps in some individuals' understanding, but also seemed to be the most successful of the three activities – the one they got most enthusiastic about. So it went okay. Big relief! And I've now got a lot of information and insight into these learners' needs. I can see I started off way too far ahead of where they were. That's why I was losing their attention for every lesson. I should have done this sort of initial assessment in my first session with them, last week. So I've learnt something useful here.

I was discussing this afterwards with Matt. I'd already come clean with him and told him the problems I'd been having.

'So this was initial assessment?' he said. 'And that's about assessing learner's needs?'

'Right', I said 'It's about finding out where they're starting from. It's sometimes called diagnostic because you're sort of diagnosing their strengths and areas they'll require more help with, and consequently the type and level of support they're going to need from you as a teacher.'

'I could see you've got some really bright ones in that group', he said. 'But you've got one or two who are having real trouble following what's going on. And one or two of the lads who avoided writing anything down. Problems with literacy, maybe?'

I hadn't noticed this, and I said so, and we had a laugh then about who was helping who.

'But how're you going to handle all this? It's a big ask, isn't it? Planning sessions that'll work for all of them?'

So we talked a bit about differentiation by task and differentiation by outcome, and he asked me if it would be alright if he sat in on a few more sessions so that he could see how this would work in practice. I feel quite comfortable about that. It's useful having someone to discuss a lesson with, even when you have to have that discussion while racing along the corridor to your next class!

Also it turns out that Matt has a really good mentor – Alia. Lucky guy. So I went over at five o'clock to see the Assistant Principal in charge of professional development to tell her I still haven't got one. She wasn't there – a bit of a relief, really, because I find her quite scary, the way she always stands a bit too close – so I left a message with her P.A. Maybe hear something tomorrow. Shan't hold my breath, though.

Section C

Wednesday

Potentially, in my view, the trickiest thing about using differentiated tasks is the problem with introducing those tasks without also planting the idea that some learners are *better* than others because they've been given something more difficult or complex to do. I've decided the best way to avoid this problem is just to set tasks that have several stages to them, from basic to more advanced and complex, so that learners can work through them up to the level at which they feel confident and competent – or maybe a little beyond, for those who enjoy stretching themselves. This approach also incorporates differentiated outcomes against which to assess them. So that, for example, if a learner manages to complete stages one and two of the task she can be assessed against those two outcomes; but if she completes all the stages, one to five, she can be assessed against all five outcomes. The key to designing these activities is to start with the easiest to achieve outcomes and then make sure they increase in complexity as the learner progresses towards the final stages of the task.

I explained all this to Matt at the beginning of the session while we were waiting for the last few learners to turn up. He was obviously interested in this idea and asked whether I'd mind if he walked around the classroom while the learners were doing the work so that he could see how they were getting on. I wasn't sure about this because I thought it might put them under pressure. They're still not sure who he is or what he's sitting in there for. But I agreed anyway because it would seem a bit rude not to. So he wandered around, peering over shoulders, asking questions and having a brief chat with one or two of them. It didn't seem to bother anybody. So I did the same. And by the end of the session I was feeling pretty pleased with myself. All that lesson planning until 2am this morning has paid off. Nice orderly classroom, all the learners getting on with their work. The only drawback is the pile of marking I'll have to do tonight.

I was a bit put out, though, when Matt and I were chatting afterwards, to hear that he'd noticed two young women playing with their phones for a lot of the time. Why didn't I spot that? It made me feel a bit of an idiot. But at least I know now, and I can have a think about what to do about it. I had some admin time, so we went down to the refectory for a coffee and had a preliminary look through the activity sheets I'd taken in. We compared two of them – one that was completed and one where the learner had only got as far as the second task. Then Matt asked an interesting question:

'So this differentiation by task sort of allows them to find their own level, right? But how do we know it's the level they're actually capable of? I mean, take those lasses who were on their phones. They probably only completed a couple of stages of this, but it wasn't necessarily because they couldn't go any further, was it? They just decided to disengage and play with their phones instead. So the assessment data you get from marking their sheet will be unreliable, won't it?'

He's right, of course. So I've got to go away and think about this. What I said to him at the time was that maybe they'd decided to play with their phones because they'd found the rest of the activity too difficult for them. He nodded politely, but we both knew that I wasn't really answering his question.

'So what will you do with these sheets when you've marked them?'

'I'll make a record of the marks', I said. 'And then I'll give the sheets back with plenty of written formative assessment, and some general verbal feedback to the whole group.'

'Okay. So when you say formative assessment, just remind me again what that means exactly.'

'Formative feedback is feedback that helps them improve their work', I said. 'It's easy to remember if you think of its purpose as being to form or shape their future performance. In that sense it's very different from assessments like final exams, where the feedback is just a grade or a percentage – a final verdict on the learner's performance. That's known as summative assessment. It's the final summary of how they've done. It's a judgement. It doesn't tell them how they can improve. Whereas formative assessment is developmental and takes the form of advice.'

I was quite proud of that explanation. I sat back and took a glug of my coffee.

'Okay', said Matt. 'Got it. So you'll just write this advice down for them on their marked worksheets? What about the ones who won't bother reading it?'

He's a bit too clever by half, is Matt.

'Well, obviously I'll give some one-to-one verbal feedback to individuals who I think need particular help or encouragement.'

'And what about to the ones who deserve particular praise. Do they need a few words too?'

'Yes, of course', I said, feeling flustered. 'I'll be giving verbal feedback to those as well.'

It's Matt's teacher training day tomorrow so he won't be sitting in with me. Good. He's beginning to make me feel as though he knows the job better than I do.

Section D

Thursday

Still no word about a mentor. I went along to see Alia this morning to ask what she thinks I should do about it. I was half hoping she'd offer to mentor me herself. It seems a bit unfair that Matt gets such a good mentor when he's only a trainee teacher, and I'm here with a full timetable, doing my first year of teaching, with no support at all. Alia said she'd chase it up for me and told me to come to her in the meantime if I have any problems or questions, which is really nice of her.

I gave the marked work back to the level 2 group this morning and spent quite a long time going over each stage of the task and making sure (I hope) that everyone understood what the correct answers were and why. I remembered to avoid the 'Everybody clear about that?' approach. When I was doing my teacher training last year I observed several teachers who used that phrase or something like it. 'Everybody got that?' or 'Anybody still not understand it?' They're such daft questions, because what young learner is going to stick their hand up and admit that they don't understand something that all the rest of the class (apparently) is completely clear about? Of course they won't! It's a completely unreliable way for the teacher to assess understanding. And I can remember promising myself at the time that I'd never use it. Instead, I used directed questioning and also invited questions, until I was pretty confident that everyone had got it. All this takes a long time, though, and I've only got a limited number of hours with the group this year to get through the required scheme of work. So I'm beginning to understand better the temptation to cut corners.

On the way home I've been thinking about a couple of the things Matt said. One was about how do we assess whether a low-achieving learner is working to their full capacity or just getting poor results because they're not trying. I think that's a really tough one to answer, and I'm going to have to reflect some more on that. And the other thing was about giving feedback to learners who've done really well. When he raised that it made me realise that I've been concentrating on the best ways to give useful, supportive and constructive feedback to the learners who need to do better in the assessment, and forgetting to make sure I give plenty of encouragement and praise to those who've done well. What a blind spot! And it's one I should have seen myself. The trouble is that there's so much to be thinking about when you're teaching full-time and trying to do it well. It's like spinning plates. I feel exhausted. Thank goodness tomorrow's Friday.

Section E

Friday

Got an email this morning from Staff Development giving me the name of my mentor. Better late than never, I suppose. Apparently she's a section head in the Business Studies

Department called Eleni. So I dropped her an email right away, introducing myself and asking for a meeting asap. I just hope it's someone I can get on with. But why Business Studies? I'm not sure why I can't have someone from my own vocational area. I'd have thought that would be more useful. But then Matt's subject is some sort of engineering and his mentor's is literacy – and that seems to work alright.

Today's lesson with the level 2 group went well. Matt sat in again – probably for the last time because Alia has organised for him to observe someone else next week. My lesson plan was built around a demonstration, followed by practicals, and then winding up with a Q&A session to make sure the learners could not only follow the procedure correctly but also explain back to me why it had to be done that way. They obviously enjoyed this *hands-on* approach. I must take advantage of this and build in more of it.

Afterwards, Matt had a whole barrage of questions for me about assessment. I had to get over to my next class in the far annex, so I asked him to walk with me while we talked. First of all he wanted to know why they all had to do the practical when it took up so much time and I'd already told him I was behind on the scheme of work. 'Couldn't you just get one or two volunteers to have a go?' he said.

'But then how else would I be able to validly assess that the rest would be capable of doing it correctly?' I said.

'Oh yeah. Validity. Run that past me again.'

'Well, an assessment is only valid if it tests the learner's ability to do what it is you're assessing them on. So, for example, if I did the demonstration and then assessed them by getting them to write me an essay about how to do it, that sort of assessment wouldn't be valid. That would only tell me whether they could write an essay about it. It wouldn't tell me whether they could actually do it.'

'So it wouldn't be a valid form of assessment, right?'

'Right', I said. 'Like a practical driving test. That's a valid form of assessment for whether you can drive safely and competently. But there are still some countries – aren't there? – where you just do a written test to get your licence. But a written test isn't a valid way of assessing whether you're a competent driver.'

He laughed. 'So stay off the road in those places, right?'

'And then there's reliability.' I was getting out of breath from walking fast and talking at the same time, but I was on a roll. I may be a new girl, but I'm the qualified teacher here and he's the trainee. 'An assessment is reliable if it generates the same outcome whoever is assessing. So, for example, those practicals they were doing just now, there was a list of competences. I gave you a copy, right?'

'Right.'

'So whether it was you or me observing, it was clear what we'd be looking for in terms of assessment. Did they do that, and that, and that? Yes? Then they've succeeded. Doesn't matter who's observing as long as the observer sticks to the assessment criteria and those criteria are clear and objective.'

'And that's what makes it reliable. Okay. Got it. So the clearer the checklist –'

'Er, the *assessment criteria*.' I admit I got a bit of a kick out of correcting him.

'Right. The clearer the assessment criteria, the more reliable the assessment, yeah?'

'That's right', I said. 'You've got it.'

He grinned at me and held out his hand. 'Well thanks, Jenni. I'll let you get on then.'

I shook his hand briefly and continued over to the annex. An interesting week. And I'm not sure who learnt most, him or me.

Part two: Critical thinking activities

Some of the tasks which follow require you to reflect on details of the journal account you've just read and to make professional judgements about teaching and learning, planning, reflection and, above all, assessment. These tasks also encourage you to consider how the situations and questions which Jenni faces might relate to, or arise in, your own experience as a teacher. Other tasks here suggest practical exercises aimed at helping you to consolidate what you have learned. In carrying out both these types of tasks you may find it useful to keep a reflective journal, as Jenni is doing; or to engage in discussion with a colleague or mentor; or – even better – both.

Activity 1

In section A of the journal extract, we learn something about the problems Jenni is having with her level 2 group, and her reasons for keeping a reflective journal. We also find that she is trying to cope in her first teaching appointment without any structured support. On the surface she seems to be doing okay, but you may find it useful to consider the following questions:

a)   How effective is her use of the time at the beginning of the lesson while she waits for the rest of the class to arrive?

b)   What does she gain by this? And what does she lose?

c)   Would you have advised her to begin the lesson on time, regardless of whether all the class was present? What reasons would you give for your answer?

d)   What are your own strategies for coping with learners' lack of punctuality? How useful or effective are they?

e)   Considering this lesson as a whole, would you have advised Jenni to do anything differently; and if so, what and why?

f) What are her reasons, as you understand them, for planning to introduce some diagnostic assessment into her next lesson with this group?

g) Reflect for a moment on your own experience of teaching so far and consider your own use of initial or diagnostic assessment of learners' current understanding and needs. Are there ways you could improve your practice? If so, what could you do differently?

Activity 2

In section B, we have Jenni's journal entry about her next lesson with the level 2 group. This time she has Matt, the trainee teacher, sitting in as observer. This lesson seems to be more successful than the previous one.

a) Why do you think this lesson works better for Jenni?

b) In your own words, explain the rationale behind her planning.

c) How do the three activities she describes help her to assess her learners' needs and current level of knowledge and understanding?

d) In your view, what are the strengths and weaknesses of these activities in terms of diagnosing individual learning needs?

e) If you had to suggest an additional or alternative activity she could use for the same purpose, what would it be, and why?

f) Jenni assumes that Matt is there to learn from her, but can you suggest at least two things that Jenni is able to learn from Matt during this session?

g) What are Jenni's reasons for introducing differentiation?

h) Think of your own most recent experience of teaching and supporting learning. Did you use differentiation in the assessment of your own learners? If so, what form did it take, and why?

Activity 3

In section C, we read about Jenni's Wednesday session with the same level 2 class and the activity she has designed in order to introduce some differentiation. Her aim is to enable each learner to work at the level most appropriate to them so that their interest remains engaged. The activity will also allow Jenni to assess each learner against the outcomes appropriate to their current attainment. She seems to regard this differentiation by task and outcome as having been a very successful strategy – until Matt raises one or two questions about it. So here are a few more questions you might find it useful to consider:

a)   To allow for differentiation, Jenni has designed an activity composed of several stages. Drawing on your own classroom experience, suggest any alternative ways she could have employed differentiated tasks and outcomes.

b)   Matt raises a crucial question about the staged activity as a means of assessing learners' knowledge and understanding. What is the question? Does it relate to the *reliability* or to the *validity* of this assessment strategy?

c)   Drawing on your own experience, suggest a way in which this potential problem could be overcome.

d)   Matt asks whether he can circulate about the classroom to observe the learners working. Jenni is reluctant at first, fearing that learners might find it intimidating. However, Matt's idea clearly pays off. How?

e)   In terms of assessment, what other advantages might there be to walking around the room rather than remaining static while learners are working?

f)   Think about the last session you taught. Roughly what proportion of time were you static or occupying only the front of the room? What were the advantages and disadvantages of this?

g)   Look again at Jenni's explanation of *formative* and *summative* assessment. Now have a go yourself at explaining the difference between these terms in one sentence of less than forty words.

h)   When Jenni and Matt discuss written formative feedback, Matt questions whether learners can be relied on to read this. In your experience, is he making a valid point here? What could Jenni do to ensure that learners *do* read and take on board any helpful feedback she writes on their work?

i)   Matt also reminds Jenni that the learners who have performed well need feedback too. In your view, should this feedback consist entirely of praise, as Jenni and Matt seem to be suggesting? To what extent should you *stretch* learners who have achieved the required outcomes by encouraging them to continue improving beyond that level?

j)   By the end of section C we get the impression that Jenni is feeling less enthusiastic about having Matt sit in as observer. Is this justified, do you think? What is the etiquette that should apply to one colleague observing another? Is it being broken here?

Activity 4

In section D, we read Jenni's account of her Thursday session with the same group. Matt isn't there for this one, but Jenni is still mulling over some of the issues he raised the day before. She also raises a new issue of her own – the disadvantages of the 'Everybody clear about that?' approach to assessment.

a) What is Jenni's objection to this approach? In your view, is it valid?

b) Think honestly about your own recent teaching. Have you found yourself asking a similar question to a class? If so, did it result in any learners asking for clarification or admitting they didn't understand?

c) What are the disadvantages of this approach in terms of reliability of assessment?

d) Jenni uses directed questioning (questions directed to named learners) instead, as a more reliable way of assessing individuals' understanding. Some would argue that this strategy, too, has its disadvantages. What do you suggest these might be?

Activity 5

In section E we have Jenni's Friday entry for her journal. It looks as though she's finally been sorted out with a mentor, and this is also her last day with Matt as an observer. She's got to grips with her level 2 group during the course of this week and conducted a successful demonstration and practical. And so altogether she's feeling fairly upbeat. We certainly get this impression as she gives Matt a mini-lecture on validity and reliability while they're crossing the campus.

a) Look again at Jenni's explanation of validity and reliability. In your view, are the examples she uses clear? Can you think of other examples, apart from the driving test, to illustrate the concept of validity in assessment?

b) How would you define these two – validity and reliability – succinctly in one sentence of less than forty words?

c) In your own experience, is the provision of assessment criteria (or competence statements) a guarantee that the assessment outcome will be identical if carried out by different assessors? Consider what evidence you could give for your answer.

d) Jenni ends her journal entry with a wry question about who has learnt most that week: Matt as observer, or herself as observed. Think for a moment about your own experiences in these two roles. Were you able to learn from both? What positive and continuing impact has either (or both) of these experiences had on your professional practice as a teacher?

And finally...

» *You will find some helpful texts relating to the topics covered in this story listed under Further Reading at the back of this book.*

» *To find out more about Jenni's mentor and whether the relationship works out or not, you'll need to read on...*

Story 3 Selecting methods and strategies

Chapter aims

This story will help you to reflect on:

- how the choice of learning and teaching methods can affect learner motivation;

- how learner engagement can be encouraged by a careful choice of activities;

- the importance of taking learning styles into account when planning a lesson;

- the advantages and disadvantages of group work;

- the importance of making learning an enjoyable experience;

- the range of roles the teacher can play, from instructor to facilitator;

- the importance of having clear learning outcomes when trying out new methods of teaching and learning;

- the needs of trainee teachers in terms of support and advice, and how they can go about obtaining these.

Part one: Matt tries out some new teaching methods

Section A

It was the third Monday of the Autumn term, the beginning of Matt's third week as a trainee teacher, and already there were leaves underfoot and a chilly wind blowing across the college campus. As he rounded the corner by the admin building he saw two police cars parked by the main entrance. Was this something to do with the money he'd found, all stuffed into a brown envelope and left unnoticed under a table after the classroom had emptied? He slowed down to a stroll. If that was what the boys in blue were there for, they'd no doubt want a statement from him. He'd taken the envelope straight over to Gail Clifford, the Assistant Principal in charge of staff development, and then heard no more about it. That was over a week ago. He'd even begun to wonder whether she'd just kept quiet about it and squirreled it away for her retirement.

There was still no movement around the police cars by the time he reached his destination – the new building everyone called the 'Pillarbox' because of its shape and bright red paint-work. He was going to be observing a different teacher this week – a bloke this time – by the name of Mo. Matt had spent the previous week observing a woman called Jenni. She was nice enough, but a bit uptight; he'd got the impression, by the end, that she was glad to see the back of him. So he was hoping that this bloke, Mo, was going to be a bit more relaxed about the whole thing. It was a level 3 group that he'd be observing Mo teach, so it'd be interesting to see what differences there were from the level 2 group he'd sat in with last week. It was a Health and Social Care class – nothing to do with his own vocational area. But his mentor, Alia, who'd set this up for him, had convinced him that this didn't matter. 'At this stage you're there to observe the teaching and learning', she'd said. 'You're not there to check out the subject content.' She was right, of course. She usually was. He bypassed the lift and took the stairs two at a time. Got to stay fit. No reason to let things go just because he was in civvies now.

Mo turned out to be a big, miserable-looking bloke in a navy blue suit. He ignored the hand Matt held out for him to shake, and nodded towards the back of the room. 'Sit yourself some-where out of the way', he said.

Matt tried a friendly smile. 'Thanks for letting me come in to observe.'

'Don't thank me. It's not like I had a choice about it.'

Great, thought Matt, and went to sit where laughing boy had directed him. Was it always like this, he wondered. That was two teachers so far not exactly welcoming him in with open arms. It must put some of the more nervous trainee teachers right off. Not him, though. He got his notepad and pencil out of his day sack. Nothing like a bit of low tech kit to get you into the classroom mood.

It was gone quarter past when the last of the learners wandered in. Unlike Jenni, Mo didn't seem to be using this waiting time for anything useful, but instead stood with his hands in his pockets, his back to the class, looking out of the window. The noise level in the room rose higher and higher. Matt was earwigging in to the conversations nearest to him, which were mainly about some TV programme. He flexed his fingers once or twice and resisted the temp-tation to call the class to order. Finally, Mo turned around and strode over to the projector.

'Right!' he said. And with no further preamble he launched into a lengthy series of slides about safeguarding. Much of the content related to legislation, and a number of the slides were densely crowded with text in a font size that required Matt to squint at them from his position at the back of the class. The deal seemed to be that the learners had to scribble down as much as they could of the slide contents before Mo cut to the next one. There never seemed to be quite enough time, even for the fastest among them, and Matt noticed that several learners gave up the effort quite early. Some didn't even continue to watch the slides but put their heads down or fiddled about with their phones. Mo didn't appear to care, or perhaps he didn't notice, because most of the time he was standing with his back turned, reading off the screen.

It was the quietest class that Matt had watched so far – but that was probably because most of the learners couldn't spare the time or energy to talk because they were too busy frantically copying the slides. The clock ticked around slowly, slowly, towards the end of the forty-minute session. Matt was waiting for a question and answer session, or a recap, or some discussion of how all this information was relevant to the learners' chosen vocational area. But the slides went relentlessly on until the very last minute of the lesson, at which point, Mo killed the projector and stood with his arms folded while the learners stampeded from the room like extras from a jailbreak movie.

Matt approached him with caution. Mo had his head down now, stuffing papers into a folder on his desk. Was this a ploy to avoid eye contact?

'Have you got a minute, mate? Just to talk me through that lesson? And thanks again for letting me sit in on it, by the way.'

Mo looked pointedly at his watch. 'Two minutes, then' he said. 'Some of us have to work.'

For a split second Matt imagined decking him. But he was a teacher now, and teachers don't do that sort of thing. Instead he thanked him again, and gestured to the projector. 'You got through a fair bit of stuff this morning', he said.

'That's right', said Mo. 'Keep 'em busy, keep 'em quiet. Job's a good 'un.'

'I noticed some of them couldn't keep up.'

'Tough', said Mo. 'They'll have to sharpen up a bit then, won't they?'

'I was wondering', said Matt, 'about differentiation. You know, because there'll be some in that group who might find it harder writing stuff down than others do.'

'And?'

'Well', said Matt, knowing better than most when it was wise to back down. 'I was just wondering about it, you know?'

Mo said nothing.

'See you tomorrow, then', said Matt.

'Apparently so', said Mo, turning back to his folder of papers.

Feeling well and truly dismissed, Matt climbed the stairs, hoping he'd find Alia in the office she shared on the next floor.

Section B

'Explain to me again why you don't want to go back in there.' This was Alia, smiling at him over her coffee mug. She'd listened carefully to Matt's account of the lesson he'd just seen. She hadn't interrupted or appeared to doubt anything he was telling her. Luckily, they had the office to themselves; but Matt was aware that colleagues could walk in at any time so he had to make this brief. He was well aware that there was a fine line here between professional concern and dropping someone in it; and he was trying hard to stay on the correct side of it.

'Well, for a start', said Matt, 'he obviously doesn't want me there. And second, what am I going to learn from it? Far as I can see, he's not doing anything right. Not anything.'

'Okay. Let's take those one at a time. So he doesn't want you there. How does that make you feel?'

Matt laughed. 'Not great. Believe me.'

'But it's part of his professional responsibility – as it is for all of us – to allow trainee teachers to observe him if a line manager has requested it. So you're entitled to be there. The question is: can you cope with him making you feel uncomfortable about it?'

'It's not just a case of feeling uncomfortable', said Matt. 'I can do uncomfortable, no worries. But the bloke was actively trying to antagonise me. He was trying to push my buttons.'

'And why do you think he was doing that?' asked Alia.

'So I wouldn't want to come back, I suppose.'

'And is that going to work with you? Or are you going to keep your professional head on, see this as a tough bit of training and stick with it?'

Matt laughed again. 'You're good!' he said. 'But what about the other problem? How can I learn anything useful about teaching from somebody who can't bloody teach?'

Alia frowned and Matt realised he'd raised his voice. So he leaned forward and said quietly, 'Sorry. But that's a genuine question.'

'I think you know the answer to that already', said Alia. 'Just think about it.'

And then Matt realised that earlier, in giving her his account of the lesson, he had followed every description of what Mo had done by telling Alia exactly how he, Matt, thought it *should* have been done. He sighed. He *had* learnt a lot from observing that session. He'd gained a much clearer understanding of what constituted poor practice, and why. His mentor was right again. As usual.

'Okay. Let me just ask you this then: Do you think I should try to talk anything through with him next time? Ask him anything about his methods? Because when I tried that today what I got from him was a very clear Back Off.'

Alia nodded and took his mug, signalling their time was up. 'All I can say is that he should be prepared to discuss his lesson with you afterwards, even if only briefly, because that's part of the deal. But it's going to be up to your professional judgement how far to take it. And I think I can trust your professional judgement, so you should too.'

Section C

The next day, Tuesday, it was raining, which seemed to capture exactly the mood in Mo's classroom when Matt arrived. About half the class was there, looking tired or glum; but there was no sign of Mo. Matt nodded to one or two of them and took his seat at the back of the room. Two girls sitting immediately in front of him turned in their seats to talk to him. They wanted to know who he was and why he was there. When he said he was there to watch their teacher, one of them turned to the other and hissed, 'I told you so.' They both kept glancing at the door, obviously keeping an eye out for Mo.

'So don't worry', said Matt, intending to put them at their ease. 'I'm not here to watch any of you. Nothing for you to worry about.'

'Will you sack him?' asked one of the girls, excitedly. They were both watching him avidly now, keen for his answer.

Matt was dumbfounded. 'Sack him?' he repeated. 'Sack who?'

But at that moment Mo walked in and the girls turned quickly, eyes front, leaving Matt to ponder just how he'd dug himself into that particular hole.

He was, however, pleasantly surprised to find that this time there was going to be no slide show. Instead, Mo marched from table to table, throwing down a set of stapled handouts on each one. 'You've got forty-five minutes', he barked at the class. 'And keep the noise down.' Then he went over to his desk and turned his attention to what appeared to be a pile of marking.

Matt peered over the shoulders of the girls in front of him. The handout was evidently a case study. There were three sheets of closely packed text to read, followed by four bullet-pointed questions, each several lines long. From what he could see, the case study had no relevance to safeguarding, so this didn't seem to be a follow-up or a consolidation of yesterday's lesson. The class was fairly quiet for some time, presumably because there was quite a lot to read. Matt wished he'd been given a copy, too. As it was, he was completely in the dark. What was this lesson about? What were the learning outcomes supposed to be? It was no comfort to realise that the learners were probably as much in the dark as he was. He toyed with the idea of joining in with one of the groups so that he could get a better idea of what was going on. But which one? And anyway he didn't want to get Mo's back up more than necessary. He shifted restlessly in his chair. Despite what Alia said, this was surely looking like a big waste of his time.

Not all of the learners were reading. Some had given up on the task already, if they'd even started it; and the noise level in the room was beginning to rise. Mo seemed unconcerned. He hadn't looked up once from his work, and Matt imagined how this made his learners feel – this lack of communication and concern. What if they had questions about the task? What if they needed help or advice with some aspect of it? What if some of them felt it was beyond them and needed a teacher's encouragement to get engaged with it? He came to a decision, left his seat and walked to the front of the room, only too aware of the interest this generated, especially from the two girls who'd spoken to him. Only Mo didn't seem to notice him, even when Matt came to a halt at his desk.

'Can you let me have a copy of the case study, mate?'

Mo didn't even glance up. 'None left', he said.

'Shall I join in with one of the groups, then?'

'No. I'd rather you didn't.'

Matt wanted to demand why not, but thought better of it. 'Could you just let me see a copy of the lesson plan then, mate? Just so I've got some idea of what's going on.'

'You must be joking', said Mo. 'I'm an experienced teacher. I don't need lesson plans. And if I had one, why would I give it to you? So you could copy it and save yourself some hard work?'

Matt was aware that the entire class was listening now. He could almost sense them holding their breath, waiting for what was going to happen next.

'To be honest', he said, pitching his voice low so that the class wouldn't overhear, 'you wouldn't have to worry about me copying your lesson plan because I'd want to take a very different approach to supporting learning. I don't see myself doing things the way you do.'

'Really?' sneered Mo. He wasn't keeping his voice low at all. 'Well perhaps you'd like to take the class tomorrow? Show us all how it's done?'

Matt frowned and lifted one hand slightly to signal that Mo needed to keep his voice down. 'Trouble is, mate, it's not my subject.'

'Right. So you don't know anything about it, but you're still happy to tell me what I should be doing.'

'Tell you what', said Matt, still keeping his voice low and reasonable. 'They have to cover first aid, right? I'll do them a session on first aid tomorrow. How about that? And', he added quickly without giving Mo a chance to respond, 'thanks for the opportunity. I'll go now and fix it up with Alia and let Gail Clifford know.' And he left the room smartly without a backward glance. He was quite pleased with himself for throwing Gail Clifford's name in there. Hopefully Mo found her just as scary as he did.

Section D

He could tell that Alia at first was horrified. But then she appeared to see some humour in it. She sent an email to Ms Space-Invader Clifford informing her that there'd been a change of plan; that Matt would be doing his first observed teaching practice (TP) with Mo's level 3 group and that she, Alia, would be observing him. She copied Mo into that one and then sent him one separately to thank him for giving Matt this opportunity.

'Okay', she said to Matt. 'All sorted. You'd better go off and get planning.'

There was no turning back now.

So this was to be his first formal teaching practice. He was going to be assessed on it, and that assessment would count one way or the other towards his chances of qualifying as a teacher. The fact that it was going to be Alia observing him didn't make it feel any easier. If anything, it piled the pressure on. Because she was such a good teacher herself, she'd be expecting only the best. Matt steeled himself and began to work out a plan. He made a couple of telephone calls. He was going to get one shot at this and he'd better make it a good one.

The following afternoon Alia waited for him outside the classroom so that they could walk in together. She was surprised to find herself feeling nervous on his behalf; but then these were rather unusual circumstances under which to do an assessed teaching session, borrowing a class from a teacher whose hostility was obvious, and rashly taking on this session as a sort of challenge. If she was feeling nervous, how must Matt be feeling?

She was surprised to see him emerge from the stairwell carrying a large suitcase. 'I see you've decided to run away', she said.

He grinned. There was no sign of nerves. 'Got a mate of mine in here', he said. 'I'll introduce you later.'

He'd produced a clear and detailed lesson plan, a copy of which she took with her to the back of the room where she settled down to observe. She was surprised – and impressed – when a copy of the same plan went up on the screen as a slide and Matt began to talk the learners through what they were going to be doing – the aim of the session, the intended outcomes, the activities they'd be carrying out and the various ways he was going to assess them against those outcomes. All the class was present and correct but there was – unfortunately – no sign of Mo. That was a great shame, thought Alia. Already he could have learnt something useful, just from Matt's lesson opener.

The topic was basic first aid. Matt quickly established his credentials by explaining that he'd gained his knowledge and experience of this as a serving soldier. He told the class that he was going to take things at a steady pace but that he was happy to pause at any time for questions or clarification. He asked whether any of them already had some knowledge of first aid, and then invited those three to help him answer any questions. Then he asked the class to guess what was in the suitcase. Every time someone made a guess he asked them their name and then used it. By the time he threw the case open and revealed a dummy head and torso to gasps of surprised laughter, he already knew the names of about a third of the learners.

When it came to the demonstration of CPR to the strains of the Bee Gees' *Staying Alive*, Alia found herself wanting to burst into applause. This session was exactly what this group had needed to remind them that learning can be fun and that teachers can feel enthusiastic about their subject and respectful towards their learners. She was impressed that Matt managed the timing so that everyone got a go. They asked sensible questions (such as what do you do if the casualty is a small child) and took notes and conferred with each other. They also all had a go at moving an unconscious body into the recovery position. Matt asked the three first aiders to be the bodies, and then got those three to demonstrate on each other. 'I have to get you all to have a go', Matt explained. 'Otherwise how can I assess whether you can do it?'

Towards the end of the session he did a recap, asked a few questions and then invited the learners to ask him anything they needed clarification about. After three or four questions a girl sitting just in front of Alia put up her hand and asked whether Matt was going to be their teacher from now on.

'I'm afraid not', he said. 'I wish I was.'

'So isn't he getting the sack, then?' said the girl.

'No.'

There was a collective groan from the class.

'That'll do', said Matt, briskly. 'Any more questions about first aid?'

At the end of the lesson the learners were slow to leave. Several of them clustered around Matt as he was packing up. Alia could hear some of them asking questions which, to her mind, were childish or inappropriate, such as had he ever been wounded and had he ever killed anyone. She wondered whether she should go to intervene, but then saw that he was perfectly in control, ignoring any questions he didn't want to answer while remaining good humoured and approachable. She regretted enormously that Mo hadn't been able to bring himself to observe this session with her. She could have discussed it with him and maybe helped him – in a tactful way – to see the contrast between what he'd seen and his own approach in terms of getting learners properly engaged and motivated. Developmentally it would have been an absolute gift for him.

'How did I do?' Matt asked her as they headed to the canteen.

'You tell me', she said, smiling.

'I thought it went pretty well, on the whole.'

'Me, too', said Alia. 'So let's get a mug of tea and talk about it.'

Part two: Critical thinking activities

The tasks that follow are designed to help you reflect on how the choice of teaching and learning methods, as well as the relationship between teacher and learners, can have a significant impact on learners' motivation and levels of engagement. They also encourage you to consider how the situations which Matt faces might relate to, or arise in, your own experience as a teacher. If you keep a reflective journal you might find it a useful place to note down your responses to these tasks. Alternatively, you might like to discuss them with a colleague or mentor.

Activity 1

a)   In section A, we read about Matt's first session observing one of Mo's lessons. Hopefully, the reception he gets is not something you've ever experienced in your own teacher training. But are there any elements of Matt's experience or perceptions here that felt familiar to you? How common do you think it is for trainee teachers to feel uncomfortable in this situation? Could this role as trainee/observer feel uncomfortable even if – as is usually the case – the experienced teacher's behaviour is appropriately professional and welcoming?

b)   Observation of an experienced teacher is a formal and integral part of many teacher training programmes. What is Matt hoping to get out of this observation experience? How does this compare to your own expectations when you yourself have observed an experienced practitioner teaching?

c)   Alia tells Matt that the observation of teaching in a different vocational area to his own can nevertheless be a valuable experience. Do you agree with her view? What are your own experiences of this, if any?

d)   We know that Matt disapproves of Mo's style of teaching. What are the specific things that Mo could be criticized for in this lesson? You might like to list these under two headings: *Relationships* and *Lesson Planning*.

e)   When you have completed your list, make a note of what you would have done differently against each point.

f)   Why do you think some learners are 'fiddling with their phones'? Think carefully about this question. The answer may be more complex than Mo would claim it to be, and an accurate answer would provide some useful insight into learner motivation.

g)   What do you think Mo means by 'Keep 'em busy, keep 'em quiet'? What does this tell you about his priorities?

h)   Towards the end of the section we realise that Matt is feeling very angry, but chooses not to show this because 'teachers don't do that sort of thing.' In your view, to what extent do (i) Matt and (ii) Mo conform to professional standards of behaviour in this situation? It's a good idea to give specific examples of behaviour to support your answer.

Activity 2

a)   Section B consists of Matt's meeting with his mentor following this uncomfortable observation. We don't hear directly or in detail what he told her about the lesson, but it's clear he's done a lot of talking and Alia, his mentor, has done a lot of listening. To what extent does this reflect your own experience of mentoring?

b) Matt gives two reasons for not wanting to continue with his observations of Mo's teaching. One is that he feels unwelcome and the other is that he doesn't think he'll learn anything from watching poor teaching. What are Alia's counter-arguments, and to what extent do you agree with them?

c) If you were in Matt's place, would you persevere, as he agrees to, or would you insist on being given an alternative option? What are the reasons for your answer?

d) Matt clearly regards Alia as a good mentor. What do you think it is about her – what she does and what she says – that leads him to value her?

Activity 3

a) In this section, we see Matt go back in and observe a second lesson taught by Mo. The situation becomes fraught. One problem is that the learners seem to misunderstand Matt's purpose in being there. What do they think his role is? How could Matt have avoided this misunderstanding? How well does he deal with the mistake when it becomes evident?

b) What would/do you say about your role if you are sitting in on a class as a trainee/ observer? In your view, is it the responsibility of the observer or of the classroom teacher to introduce the observer to the class? Should the observer have some say in how they are introduced? (For example, some people might want to avoid being categorized as a trainee teacher this early in their college experience.)

c) There is a clue in this section that the learners are quite nervous of Mo. Did you spot the evidence for that?

d) From the learners' point of view, what does Mo's behaviour say about his attitude towards them? It would be useful to cite specific examples of his behaviour in your answer.

e) Matt describes the handout to us. From the information he gives us, how would you evaluate its design as a level 3 resource?

f) Mo tells Matt: 'I'm an experienced teacher. I don't need lesson plans.' Have you ever been told this by an experienced teacher? How would you persuade someone that every teacher needs lesson plans? What specific arguments would you use?

g) There is a very uncomfortable stand-off between Matt and Mo towards the end of this section. Again, in your view, to what extent do (i) Matt and (ii) Mo conform to professional standards of behaviour in this situation? It is a good idea to give specific examples of behaviour to support your answer.

Activity 4

a)   This section opens with Alia formalizing the arrangements for Matt's TP. What do her actions tell you about her?

b)   Matt begins his session by going through the lesson plan with the learners. What are the advantages of doing this?

c)   Alia is pleased to see that Matt establishes his credentials. Why is this important? How do you establish your own credentials with learners? Could you do this more effectively?

d)   Matt tells the learners he is happy to pause at any time for questions or clarification. This is a difficult promise to make when you are trying to stick to a time constrained lesson plan. How do you yourself balance these two priorities – time and learner needs – in your own teaching?

e)   Matt identifies learners who already have some knowledge of the topic. Why was this important? Does he make effective use of this information, and if so, how? Is there any other way he could have taken advantage of their expertise?

f)   He makes an opportunity to learn some of the learners' names. Why do you think he does this? How much priority do you give to learning and using learners' names?

g)   Matt explains that he needs all the learners to *have a go,* otherwise he won't be able to assess whether they've met the learning outcomes. Being able to do this very much depends on the teacher's choice of learning and teaching methods. Mo's interminable slide show, for example, doesn't create any opportunity for assessment. How do you address this issue in your own lesson planning?

h)   It seems the learners still think Matt's role is somehow connected with getting rid of, or replacing Mo. How does Matt handle this question when it crops up again at the end of the session? If you found yourself in the position of hearing criticism of another teacher from your learners, how would you handle it?

And finally...

»   *You will find some helpful texts relating to motivating learners and making a choice of learning and teaching methods listed under Further Reading at the back of this book.*

»   *To find out whether there are any repercussions from Matt's face-off with Mo, and whether Matt hears any more about that envelope of cash, you'll need to read on...*

Story 4 Motivating learners and encouraging appropriate behaviour

Chapter aims

This story will help you to reflect on:

- the immediate causes of learner disengagement within the context of a lesson;

- the links between motivation and behaviour;

- useful strategies to encourage learners to engage with their learning;

- the importance of careful planning to optimise learner motivation and engagement;

- the distinction between disengagement and non-compliance;

- useful strategies for addressing non-compliance and encouraging appropriate behaviour;

- the needs of a newly qualified teacher in terms of support, advice, a listening ear and an experienced and competent role model.

Part one: Jenni encounters some bad behaviour

Section A

Jenni was curled up in armchair at home with the laptop on her knee and a large bar of chocolate on the table beside her. It was dark outside and still raining. She sighed miserably and pecked out a few words on the keyboard:

Tuesday
Third week of term. Terrible day. It started when I went to see my mentor, and then just went downhill from there.

She broke off a piece of chocolate and ate it. It didn't make her feel any better; but she ate another bit anyway. What a day!

She'd arrived at work early so that she could pop over to Business Studies to meet her mentor for the first time. Eleni turned out to be older than Jenni had expected – around her mother's age, perhaps – and quite glamorous-looking. She greeted Jenni warmly, even giving her a hug, and then handing her a mug of tea.

'Sit down', she said, waving Jenni into a comfy chair at the side of her work station. 'I've just got to finish checking these emails.'

She was checking them on her phone, not her work computer, which sat silent, screen blank, on her desk. She was manipulating her phone not with her thumbs, but by prodding and poking at it painstakingly with one perfectly manicured finger. Jenni had seen her mother do the same. Maybe it was a generation thing.

Jenni sipped her tea. Five minutes went by. Surreptitiously, she checked her watch. Her first class started in a quarter of an hour and she couldn't be late. She'd not met them before. She'd got them today because their timetabled teacher had gone sick. There'd been some suggestion on the grapevine that his absence was due, in part at least, to the behaviour of this class, so Jenni was already feeling apprehensive. She looked at her watch again and cleared her throat.

'Er, I've got a class starting at nine, so um...'

'Sorry!' said Eleni. 'Sorry. Nearly finished. Have you ever done this? I think it must be a bit addictive.' And she laughed.

'What's that?' Jenni asked.

'Online dating.'

Jenni stared at her mentor, but her mentor was still focused on her phone. Finally she put it down and turned her attention to Jenni with a smile. 'I was hoping there'd be an email from this man I've been seeing. Nic. Nic with a 'C'. We've been getting along so well. I think I've fallen for him, to tell you the truth. This online dating is a marvellous thing. He's the nicest one I've met by far. I don't know why he hasn't emailed. I'll check again later.'

'I just wanted to introduce myself, really', said Jenni, 'and to maybe fix a time –'

'Are you single?'

'Well, yes. What –'

'You ought to try this online dating. It's fantastic. Since my husband died last year I must have met – oh – at least fifteen men.'

'Oh. Well. That's ... great', said Jenni. 'I don't think I'd really like it, though. Anyway, like I was saying, I wondered whether we could arrange a time –'

'There's nothing wrong with it', said Eleni. She'd stopped smiling and was looking a bit put out. 'There's nothing wrong with taking the initiative to get your life back on track.'

'No', said Jenni. 'Yes. No. You're right. It's probably a really good thing. But at the moment I'm concentrating on my career. Anyway, I wondered whether we could fix up a time for you to come and watch me teach?'

Eleni's phone rang. She pounced on it. Jenni checked her watch again. 'I'll have to go', she said. 'Sorry.' But Eleni was smiling into her phone and seemed to have forgotten she was there.

So I rushed across for my class, wrote Jenni, stabbing at her keyboard. *And I don't know what was making me feel worse: intense anxiety about what these learners were going to be like, or outrage that my so-called mentor couldn't drag herself away from her romantic entanglement just for five minutes so she could find out about me and get to know a bit about the support I might need. Nic with a 'C' indeed! And then I got to the classroom. And it was far, far worse than I'd even imagined.*

Section B

There was no one there. And at first Jenni wondered, in panic, whether she'd got the wrong room. Then four or five learners straggled in. They were all boys.

Or should that be 'young men'? wrote Jenni in her journal. *I'm never sure what the appropriate term is, but 'young men' and 'young women' makes this lot sound a bit too respectable. They were 17- and 18-year-olds and they were a bit of a rabble, really, just like the rest that wandered in later, in twos and threes.*

Jenni greeted the learners as they came in. She did her best to keep a friendly smile fixed on her face, but during the long wait for the last few to arrive, the noise in the classroom rose to a level beyond the normal expected chatter. There was whooping and loud, braying laughter which she could only interpret as being confrontational and designed to test her response. It was difficult to make herself heard in order to get the lesson started. In the end she resorted to clapping her hands.

'Oooo!' shouted one of the boys. 'She's clapping us already and we haven't done owt!' This was greeted with a wave of laughter, even though it wasn't, as far as Jenni could see, particularly funny.

'Er, that'll do', she said loudly. 'Settle down. You and you –' she pointed to two learners who had seated themselves with their backs to her –'move your chairs around and face the front.' She knew this was an important point. She had to be able to make eye contact with everyone if she was to successfully establish some sort of control. 'Come on', she said, when no one moved. 'Quickly. We need to get on.'

'I'm comfy here, miss, thanks', said one of them. The other just put her head down on the table. Neither of them showed any sign of moving.

The noise level in the room had dropped a bit, but Jenni was well aware that was because the rest of the class was watching now with interest to see who won this one. Surely, she told herself, it *had* to be her.

'I don't care whether you're comfy or not', she said. 'Move. Now.'

> *When I realised they weren't going to move – either of them – it was a horrible feeling,* she wrote. *I just went into a panic. I forgot everything I'd learnt and read about classroom control and how to get learners on your side. I just thought to myself, Okay, I've got to get on. I'm just going to get on with the lesson. It was a stupid reaction, I realise that now. Because I could go through the paces as much as I liked, but if the learners weren't onside they weren't going to be learning anything. All that would be going on was teaching. But no learning. It's weird how you can understand a thing like that afterwards but not see it at the time.*

The panic had made her mind go blank. She picked up her lesson plan to remind herself of how she'd intended to start the lesson. Her hand was shaking and she didn't want the learners to see, so she put the lesson plan down again.

'Okay', she said, raising her voice above the hubbub. 'Let's start off with a few questions to see where you're up to.' But the only learner to respond to any of the questions was a girl sitting quietly right at the front who kept raising her hand. It was so comforting to get any kind of response from anyone that Jenni allowed the question and answer session to turn into a dialogue between herself and that one learner while chaos reigned in the rest of the classroom.

The lowest point of the lesson, for Jenni, was when she heard one learner – it was a girl – shout out a stream of abuse about something she'd seen on television, and in such filthy language that Jenni felt she just had to intervene. So she shouted over at the girl, 'Er, WHAT did you say?'

As soon as the question was out of her mouth she realised her mistake. Right on cue the girl repeated her outburst exactly, word for word, to the delight of the rest of the class.

> *I don't know how I got through the rest of that lesson,* wrote Jenni. She broke herself off another piece of chocolate. *Really it was just me and the girl in the front row. I was sort of kidding myself that I was doing my job of teaching because at least she was listening and seeming to get something out of it. But I can't go back in there again. I just can't. I need some help. I shouldn't have been given a class like that, not as a newly qualified teacher, not without some sort of guidance about how to handle them. If their original teacher really has gone sick because of them, then the college shouldn't just think they can solve the problem by putting an inexperienced teacher like me in there to fill the gap. That might make it look fine and sorted on paper, but it's not fair on the learners and it's not fair on me. And who can I go to for support when my mentor turns out to be some sort of obsessive silver surfer? All I can think to do is to go and see if I can find Alia tomorrow. She might be able to advise me, at least.*

Section C

'But Eleni's a really good teacher', Alia was saying. Jenni had tracked her down the next day and was having one of those conversations she was getting used to, where you try to discuss something important while hurrying down a corridor with both of you racing to be on time for your next lesson.

Jenni was in a quandary. She feared it would be unprofessional to tell Alia her real concern about Eleni. It would sound like criticism. Well, let's face it, she thought, it *would* be a criticism. But, apart from that, she wasn't sure how much of what Eleni had told her had been disclosed in confidence.

'Yes, I'm sure she's a good a teacher', she said to Alia now. 'But I'm not sure she's got time to listen to me.'

'And I have?' said Alia. And then she laughed, to take the sting out of her words. 'Listen, Jenni. Just ask her for some advice about this class of yours. Tell her what you've told me, that you need to see them being taught by an experienced teacher so that you can get some ideas about how to handle them. Email her. If you don't hear back from her today, let me know and I'll chase her up. Okay?'

Jenni thanked her and they parted at a fork in the corridor, each to their own class. It was a Wednesday, a good day for Jenni. She liked all her Wednesday classes. She would email Eleni at lunchtime, though she couldn't help wishing she had her private email address. Because at least that would probably guarantee that, in the search for word from Nic-with-a -C, her own message would come promptly to Eleni's attention.

When she checked her emails at the end of the day she was pleasantly surprised to find that Eleni had already replied.

> *Are you free first session tomorrow (Thursday)? If you are, you could come over here and watch me teaching our own class from hell. There may be one or two tips you could pick up. We'll be in P103. Feel free. Eleni*

As it happened, Thursday mornings were Jenni's only late start, because she was timetabled to teach from 10am until the end of the evening session at 9pm. But a chance to learn something useful to get her out of this pickle was a fair swap for a bit of a lie-in. Personally, she couldn't imagine Eleni's class really being worse than hers. If it was, surely Eleni wouldn't want anyone in there to see it. Not unless she was on top of it already and not having any trouble with them. Jenni felt her hopes rise. Perhaps she'd been too quick to write off Eleni as a mentor.

The next morning she presented herself at room P103 and found Eleni was already there.

'I like these 9am sessions', Eleni said. 'You can arrive in plenty of time because you're not rushing from an earlier class in some other building. And it's a new day and nobody's had a chance to get bored or fed up. Don't you think?'

Jenni nodded. 'Where shall I sit?'

'Anywhere you like. Somewhere where you can see everything going on.'

Jenni was making her way towards the back of the room when Eleni called her back to hand her the lesson plan. 'You'll need this', she said, 'so you can follow what's going on. But I need to explain one or two things to you before they get here, okay? The first thing is that I've set up a system of incentives with this group. There's the incentive to get here on time so that we don't have a messy start. Messy starts are fatal with a difficult class. Unless you've got their attention and established your role as leader from the beginning, things degenerate quickly. So the incentive I use is that if everyone's here on time, I allow music on while they're working on group tasks. They like working to music, so there's a lot of peer pressure on them to be punctual. One person arriving late with no valid reason and no apology means no music. And I stick to that absolutely. And their disappointment is aimed at the latecomer, not at me. So it's win-win.'

Jenni had taken out her notepad and was frantically trying to get all this down.

'The other incentive', said Eleni, 'is to do with completing group tasks in class. If all the groups remain on task and get the required work done, to a reasonable standard, they all get to leave the classroom fifteen minutes early from our Friday afternoon session to have some library time. They don't use it as library time, of course, most of them. They use it to get an early start on their weekend. But that doesn't matter. What matters is that – mostly – they stay on task and get the work done, because again there's very effective peer pressure on them not to cause everyone to miss out on an early Friday finish. The huge benefit to them is that they're going to be on track to succeed and to get their qualification and to think of themselves as winners instead of losers.'

'So it's a Behaviourist model, then?' said Jenni. 'A system of rewards.'

Eleni nodded. 'Right. A system of rewards where they themselves are responsible if sanctions are imposed. And there are some other strategies – more of a Humanist approach – that are important, like modelling respect and always displaying a sense of humour. But, look, they're going to arrive any minute, so I'll leave you to identify all that sort of thing for yourself.'

Jenni thanked her and settled herself at the back of the room. She noticed that although the tables were arranged in groups, all the chairs were set to face the front of the room; and she suspected that Eleni had arrived early partly to arrange them that way. So much more sensible than trying to get learners to shift to face front once they were seated. Why, oh why hadn't she thought of that on Terrible Tuesday?

The learners began to arrive and, sure enough, by nine o'clock they were all there. Eleni was smiling at them as they came in and sat down. She looked relaxed and pleased to be in their company. Will I ever look that relaxed? thought Jenni. Especially when there's someone sitting there to observe me.

'Good morning, people', Eleni was saying. 'Lovely to see you all. And it looks as though it's going to be a music day today.'

There was some cheering and some whooping, but it sounded different somehow to the racket Jenni's Tuesday class had made, perhaps because there seemed nothing aggressive or confrontational about it.

'Now, before we start', continued Eleni, 'I just want to introduce our visitor.' Heads craned round and Jenni found herself under scrutiny from about twenty pairs of eyes. She smiled awkwardly and raised her fingers in something like a wave. 'Jenni's a colleague of mine and she's heard about how well you work and she's come along to see for herself. So while you're working in your groups, as you will be a bit later, she may have a wander around so that she can see what you're doing. Let's remember she's a guest and make her feel at home. Okay? Now, let's just have a quick quiz to go over what we did last time. Two teams...' And the lesson was under way, picking up pace as it went, so that the learners never found an idle moment to stray off-task. For every activity Eleni gave them a tight time limit and regular reminders of time ticking down to the deadline. During the group tasks, with some great music playing as a background, Eleni moved from group to group, observing, praising, asking and answering questions. Jenni noticed particularly that her expression was always animated, always enthusiastic. She never appeared to be off-task herself, even for a moment; and it was clear that this was conscious and intentional. It was part of her strategy. Because what she was doing was modelling for the learners the behaviour and attitude that she expected from them.

Jenni took note particularly of the way Eleni called learners to order. This was where she herself had fallen down most badly. She noticed that Eleni never issued a direct order. Instead she phrased these sorts of interactions as requests. To one boy, for example, who was fiddling with his phone, she said, 'I'd like you to put that phone away now, Jaden, before you risk losing the whole group an early finish on Friday.' And then she moved straight on to another group without looking back, making clear her expectation that Jaden would comply. And he did, though this was clearly to some extent because of the glares he was getting from other learners. There was no doubt that Eleni's classroom management was skilfully done.

That evening, writing up her journal, Jenni allowed herself a bit of humour at Eleni's expense.

> *I'm just so impressed,* she wrote. *And I can see there's a big advantage to having Eleni as my mentor. But I can't help imagining using one of her favourite strategies on her and saying: 'I'd like you to put that phone away now, Eleni, and take some notice of me, before you risk me taking it off you and chucking it out of the window!!!'*

Section D

It was Friday lunchtime, and Jenni had been thinking long and hard about what she had learnt from watching Eleni. Last night, she'd made a bullet point list in her journal:

Thursday: What I learnt from observing Eleni

- *Use 'incentives' (ie rewards) – but they've got to be (a) feasible and (b) important enough to the learners.*

- *Be a role model for the sort of behaviour I want from the learners: cheerful, punctual, engaged, respectful, etc.*

- *Treat them with respect (treat them like adults?).*

- *Avoid giving direct orders because they can lead to confrontation. Phrase these as requests instead.*

- *Keep up the pace. Give clear parameters for timing of tasks.*

- *Move about the room, interacting one-to-one.*

This is all really useful, she wrote. *But the problem is I still don't know how Eleni got the learners to the stage I saw them at, where they were incentivised, engaged and reasonably compliant. I'm not convinced that I can go back into that Terrible Tuesday class and recover all the ground I've lost. If I'd known then what I know now, I'd have made a much better job of getting those learners motivated and onside. But now they see me as a teacher who has no control. I'm not sure it's possible to move forward from that position – and I'm still not convinced the college, or whoever does the timetabling, should have put me in that position in the first place.*

She swallowed her last bite of sandwich and looked at her watch. Twenty-five minutes until her next class – just time enough to have a word with her mentor and see whether she could do something about replacing the Terrible Tuesday lot on her timetable with groups more appropriate to her beginner status.

Over in Business Studies she found Eleni by the photocopier. Her mentor greeted her warmly like a long-lost friend.

'I'm still in awe of how you handled that class', said Jenni. 'It was *so* helpful to me to see that. But I just don't think –'

Eleni's phone chirruped and she grabbed it from her bag. 'I don't believe it!' she said. 'Do you know what he's saying now? That he doesn't want any commitment. How can he say that? I've never made any demands on him. What the hell does he mean, "no commitment"?' She began prodding at her phone with the sort of expression she'd probably wear if she was giving Nic-with-a-C a poke in the eye.

Jenni tried again. 'The thing I wanted to ask you was whether –'

'I mean, we've been getting along fine. Why does he suddenly want to spoil it all? I've never made any demands on him –'

'No', said Jenni. 'So you said. Well, I'll be off, then.'

How was it, she wondered, that someone with such skill and common sense in one area of their professional life could be so completely unself-aware when it came to relationships, whether that was with flaky men or with a mentee who had important questions to ask.

So the bottom line, wrote Jenni in her journal that evening, *is that I'm still stuck with that Tuesday class. No-one's going to come and rescue me, so I'm just going to have to cope as best I can and treat it as a learning experience (gulp!). Looking on the positive side, I suppose if I'd actually persuaded Eleni to get that class taken off my timetable it would be a sort of defeat. I'd always see it as a failure – something I'd chickened out of. And it wouldn't be*

*good for the learners, either, because if I never came back they would assume they'd suc-
ceeded in frightening me away, and that would give them the impression that they had the
power to control who was going to teach them. That would be very destructive. They would
try the same thing again – especially if, as Alia suggested yesterday, they play up like that to
avoid doing work because they're scared it'll be beyond them.*

*She also said something useful about the difference between disengagement and non-com-
pliance. She said that disengaged learners don't seem to want to learn, but don't necessarily get confrontational about it; but that non-compliant learners actively refuse to do as the
teacher asks and that turns easily into confrontation. She said that one of the most important things with a difficult class is not to create a situation where disengaged learners are
pushed over into non-compliance. That's exactly what I did when I told those two learners to
move their chairs so that they were facing the front. That's where I really lost the class. And
there are ways I could have done that differently. I could have sorted the seating out before
they got there, like Eleni did. Or I could have phrased things differently – made it a request
instead of an order.*

*Loads to think about, and a lot of planning to do. But I'm going to persevere. For now, thank
goodness it's the weekend!*

Part two: Critical thinking activities

Some of the tasks which follow require you to reflect on Jenni's experiences and to make
professional judgements about teaching and learning, planning, reflection and, above all,
learner motivation and behaviour. These tasks also encourage you to consider how the situations and questions which Jenni faces might relate to, or arise in, your own experience as
a teacher. In working through these tasks you may find it useful to keep a reflective journal, as Jenni is doing; or to engage in discussion with a colleague or mentor; or – even
better – both.

Activity 1

In this first section we see Jenni meeting her mentor for the first time.

a)   Judging from this initial meeting, how would you rate Eleni as a mentor, and why?
What strengths does she have? Would these, in your view, outweigh the weaknesses
that Jenni finds so disappointing?

b)   Consider your own experience of being mentored. What did you hope for in a mentor,
and why? What strengths did your mentor have, and how well did these match with
your needs?

c)   How professional do you consider the behaviour of (i) Jenni and (ii) Eleni at this first
meeting? Is there anything you would have done or said differently in Jenni's place?

Activity 2

In this section we have an account of Jenni's first experience with her Tuesday class. As you consider the questions that follow, think about any similar class you have experienced, as a teacher, as a learner, or as an observer, and think about what reasons might underlie the learners' behaviour here.

a) Jenni wonders whether to describe some of the learners as *boys* or as *young men*. What term do you use, and why?

b) The learners arrive late and straggle in. How could Jenni have used this time more productively? How do you use intervals like this when they arise in your teaching?

c) Jenni calls the group to order by clapping her hands. What other strategies could she have used? How do you call a class to order, or attract learners' attention when you need to speak to the class? What are the advantages and disadvantages of your strategy?

d) A learner makes a joke about her clapping which Jenni doesn't find funny. Could she have responded differently to this? If so, how? And how would you yourself have responded in a similar situation?

e) Describe four things that Jenni could have handled differently in order to get the class onside.

f) At what point, in your view, does she finally lose control of the class, and why? Can you suggest some strategy she could have used to recover from this situation and proceed productively with the lesson?

g) What do you think she means when she writes in her journal: '*All that would be going on was teaching. But no learning*'? Have you ever experienced or observed teaching where no learning was taking place? If so, why was that happening?

h) Judging from the brief extracts of her journal that we read in this section, is Jenni writing (i) reflectively or (ii) descriptively?

Activity 3

In section C, we suddenly see Eleni in a new light. We also see Jenni learning a great deal very quickly. But not everything in this section is as straightforward as it seems, and you may want to take some time to consider your answers to the following questions:

a) Jenni feels it would be unprofessional of her to tell Alia the full story of her meeting with Eleni. Why do you think she feels this way? Decide whether you agree with her, and why.

b) There is a clue in this section that Alia is beginning to feel that too many demands are being made of her. Did you spot it? Think for a moment about your own early experiences as a teacher or trainee teacher. Did you ever feel you were making too many demands on colleagues? If so, what gave you this impression? In your view, is the issue of peer support an interpersonal one or an institutional one? (In other words, is it the college or is it individuals within it who should be responsible for ensuring that peer support works effectively?)

c)   From the evidence of this section alone, how would you rate Eleni as a mentor? How does this compare with your evaluation of her in section B? If these two evaluations differ, what issues does this raise about what constitutes good mentoring support?

d)   We see Eleni hand Jenni a copy of her lesson plan. Why does she think this will be useful to Jenni as an observer? In your own experience of observing experienced teachers, do you find a copy of the lesson plan useful, and why?

e)   Eleni has set up a system of *incentives* to motivate the learners. This is based on Behaviourist theories of reinforcing required behaviour through the use of reward. She also tells Jenni that she has drawn on Humanist theory, too, in recognising that people learn more effectively when they feel valued and respected by their teacher. Can you find two examples in this account of Eleni's lesson where she is demonstrating this Humanist approach?

f)   One of the incentives or rewards for the learners is being allowed music while they work. Another is to allow them *library time* on Friday afternoon, which is really permission to leave early. What is your view about both of these? Would they be workable in your own classes? Would your college policy allow them? They clearly work for Eleni, but could have disadvantages. What might these be? Can you think of two rewards that would work better for your own learners?

g)   Eleni's strategies allow her to use peer pressure to motivate the learners. Consider carefully how she set this up. Could you usefully incorporate this motivating principle into your own teaching, and if so, how?

h)   Notice how Eleni introduces Jenni to the class. Why do you think she chooses these words to introduce her?

i)   Identify four strategies that Eleni uses which you would describe as good practice. What can you learn from these for your own teaching?

Activity 4

In section D, we see Jenni reviewing what she has learnt from observing her mentor teach, and we see her trying and failing to get the Tuesday class removed from her timetable. Finally, we read in her journal where she reflects on the problem and comes to a decision.

a)   Jenni has made a list of Eleni's strategies that she feels she can learn from. Are there any that she could have added here?

b) In your view, how do the extracts from Jenni's journal in this section compare to those we saw in section B, in terms of how reflective she's being?

c) She confides to her journal that she's not convinced she can go back into the Tuesday class after what has happened. To what extent do you agree with her argument here? Have you ever found yourself in a similar difficult position? If so, how did you resolve it?

d) She refers repeatedly to the class as the '*Terrible Tuesday class*'. What might be the disadvantages of labelling a class in this way? Have you seen this sort of labelling happen in your own professional experience?

e) Jenni decides to go ahead and try again with the difficult class. What argument/s does she use to persuade herself? Do you think she is right?

f) How would you define the difference between disengagement and non-compliance in your own words?

g) Do you agree with Jenni's diagnosis of the point at which she lost control of the class? If not, what would you identify as the tipping point?

And finally...

» *You will find some helpful texts relating to motivating learners and managing behaviour, and to writing reflectively about incidents such as these, listed under Further Reading at the back of this book.*

» *To find out what happens with that Tuesday class, and whether Jenni copes with her mentoring situation, you'll need to read on...*

Story 5 Inclusion, equality and diversity

Chapter aims

This story will help you to reflect on:

- how you can identify and evaluate issues of inclusion and equality within a group of learners;

- how issues of inclusion can arise within a class;

- your responsibilities as a teacher when dealing with bullying or bigotry;

- useful strategies to encourage learners to engage with their learning;

- the importance of careful planning to optimise inclusion;

- the importance of providing, by your own behaviour and attitudes, a role model of tolerance, fairness and equality;

- how bullying may reflect a wider, institutional ethos;

- strategies for encouraging learners to respect and value diversity;

- how to recognise your own needs as a teacher in terms of support, advice on issues of inclusion, equality and diversity.

Part one: Matt encounters bullying

Section A

Eight-thirty on a Monday morning and Matt is standing outside the office door of Gail Clifford, aka the Space Invader, Assistant Principal for staff development. He's waiting for the green light to come on, which will indicate that he is allowed to knock and enter. At the moment, the display panel at the side of her door is showing a red light. This, the notice informs him, means that she is currently busy and not to be disturbed. He wonders what she's busy doing at this time of the morning. He knows what he'd be doing if he wasn't standing here like a prat; he'd be necking a coffee and a doughnut and having a final read through his lesson plan. He's flying solo today. Alia is away at a conference and she's entrusted him with her level 3 group. He doesn't know whether to be flattered or terrified. But at the moment he's completely occupied by feeling irritated. He went through all the palaver of making an appointment. She's supposed to see him at 8.30 and it's now – he consults his watch – 8.37, and time is ticking. He needs to be over there setting the room up by 8.50.

It's been four weeks since he handed that envelope of cash in, and he's heard nothing more about it. How unlikely is that? No one's asked to speak with him – not the police, not the college authorities, no one. So what's she done with it? If it's all sorted out – whatever it is – then surely out of courtesy he should have been told. And that's why he's here, hanging about outside her door and feeling like a complete tosser every time someone walks along the corridor and glances at him.

He's just about to give up and go when the door opens and who should emerge but the guy he observed and whose class he took a week or so ago: Mo. He's wearing a smart, grey, new-looking suit instead of his customary shiny blue one, but his gut hangs over the belt just the same. When he sees Matt his initial look of surprise is quickly replaced by a malicious smile. 'Better start looking for another place to teach, Mr Lesson Plan Man', he hisses. 'Cos you're not going to be here much longer.' And stepping smartly out of reach he disappears off down the corridor, casting just one nervous look behind to make sure Matt isn't after him.

Matt hesitates for a moment. What was that all about? The light's still on red but he decides to ignore it. He knocks on the half-open door and walks in. Gail Clifford is sitting behind her desk. She looks up as he enters and she doesn't smile. Nor does she invite him to sit down. She just looks at him and he has to resist stamping to attention in front of her desk. Instead he stands easy and tries a smile.

'Thanks for seeing me', he says.

Her reply is a bit of a shock. 'I've been hearing some very troubling things about your behaviour here', she says, still eyeballing him. 'I'm afraid they cast some grave doubt on your ability to behave in an appropriate and professional manner. You are a trainee teacher. We gave you a placement here as a favour to you and as a courtesy to your tutors.' She leans forward, as though she could invade his space even from behind a desk. 'A *trainee* teacher. That is your status. And with it goes an expectation that you will behave accordingly. Do you understand?'

Matt feels as though he's been punched in the gut, but he returns her look levelly and doesn't show it.

'I do understand my status here', he says, quietly. 'And I think I understand what's expected of me. But I don't understand what it is that you're accusing me of doing. Or not doing. If I've overstepped my position or my role in some way, I need to know how. And obviously I'll apologise.'

'Discourtesy to an experienced member of our college staff is absolutely inexcusable', says Clifford.

Matt is frowning. He's beginning to work out what's happened and he's telling himself not to panic.

'Attempting to turn learners against their own teachers by questioning and belittling those teachers is both unacceptable and highly unprofessional', Clifford goes on. 'I would go so far as to say that anyone who would do that is not cut out to be a teacher. We would not give such a person a reference, and without a reference from your teaching placement it is highly unlikely that you would ever gain employment as a teacher in the sector.'

'Okay', said Matt. He squared his shoulders. 'So I'm guessing Mo has made a complaint against me.'

Clifford just fixes him with a steely stare.

'I think you need to speak to my mentor to get an accurate idea of what happened', he says. 'I did sit in on a couple of Mo's classes. I know he was reluctant to have me in there. And then he offered to let me teach the class myself for a full session. He didn't attend, but Alia, my mentor, was there the whole time observing me. She can vouch for my behaviour. I don't know what his problem is with me, but –'

'He is a full-time member of our staff. It's his word against yours, I'm afraid.'

'Please.' He hates pleading. 'Just talk to Alia.' And then he remembers and his heart sinks – Alia is away today, attending that conference.

But Clifford doesn't miss a trick. 'I'll speak to her tomorrow when she's back on campus', she says. 'In the meantime, consider this both a first and final warning.'

With a wave of the hand she dismisses him. He turns and leaves the room in a bit of a daze. The door closes behind him and the red light glares at him. And still he's no wiser about what happened to all that money.

Section B

He leaves the building and walks across to the science block, trying to get his mind focused on Alia's A level Science group. She usually has them for communication skills this morning and he's covering that class for her. There's nothing he can do at the moment about Mo's accusations and Clifford's threats, so he locks them away in the compartment of his brain marked 'Sort this later', and concentrates on the job. This class is level 3 standard. It's going to keep him on his toes. Alia's been a great mentor so far and he doesn't want to let her down. He's spent a long time on his lesson plan, making sure there's plenty of learner activity, plenty of opportunities for him to get a measure of the class, the range of ability and their progress towards the learning objectives. He's starting them off by getting them to look at a 'terms and conditions' contract for a smartphone. Then he'll ask them questions about it which raise various scenarios. It's a comprehension exercise, really – but one that he hopes will tie in with their enthusiasms and interests.

He's a couple of minutes late, and when he gets to the classroom the learners are all there, all twenty-five of them – the largest class he's taught so far. The majority are 18–19-year-olds, but there are also three older learners sitting together by the window: two women and a man. They look to be somewhere in their thirties. The rest of the class is a fairly even mix of male and female learners who, he is surprised to see, seem to have segregated them-selves according to gender: the boys at two tables of five and the girls at two tables, one of six and one of four. In addition, there are two learners – one male and one female – sit-ting at tables by themselves. The six girls who sit together are making a lot of noise. They are examining one another's nail decorations and shrieking with laughter. Five of them are wearing the hijab. Their laughter is infectious, and Matt finds himself smiling. Then he notices that one of the adult women learners is frowning in disapproval, so he quickly calls the class to order.

'Okay, people', he says. 'Let's make a start. My name is Matt and I'm covering for Alia today while she's away at a conference. I've been looking forward to meeting you all, and the first thing I need to do is to get to know some names. So we'll go round the class and what I'd like you to do is to introduce to me the person sitting on your left. Okay? If there's no-one on your left I'll point out to you who to introduce. Right. Let's go.' He points at the male adult learner. 'Let's start with you, sir.' The man introduces the woman on his left – the one Matt saw frowning – as Celia. She introduces the girl sitting alone as Bronte; and the introductions proceed smoothly from there. Until they hit a problem. To the left of the final girl on the table of six is the boy who sits alone.

'Can't introduce him', she says. 'Don't know his name, innit?'

The boy is staring down at his table. His ears have gone red.

'I can tell you what *we* call him', says Hanni, one of the other six. The others at her table shriek and laugh and wave their hands at her and tell her to shut up.

'Would you like to introduce yourself, mate?' offers Matt. What's happening isn't good and he realises he has to shut it down quickly. But the boy says nothing. He doesn't even look up. 'Don't worry about it', says Matt quickly. 'I don't blame you, mate.' And then, pointing to the final table of boys, he says, 'Right, lads. Last but not least. Go.'

When the introductions are finished, he explains the first task to them. He tells them they're going to read the smartphone contract carefully and that he's then going to ask them some *what if* questions about it. They're going to work in groups to find the correct answer, and the group with the most right answers will be the winners. He doesn't hand out the photocopied contracts until he's given the explanation. He needs them to listen and not be reading while he's talking. Then he starts sorting them into groups. He doesn't want to put the isolated boy in as the only one in a group of girls because he guesses this might be embarrassing for him. But he's obviously already chosen not to sit with the other lads. So Matt goes over while everyone's reading the handout and asks him which group he'd like to work with.

The lad doesn't make any eye contact. He keeps his head down and says, 'Can I work on my own?'

'What's your name, mate?'

'Oliver.'

'Listen, Oliver. I need you to join one of these teams. I don't want to put you where you're not comfortable, okay? How about if you join those three over there?' He nods towards the adult learners.

Oliver gets up without a word and carries his bag and handout over to the adults' table. Matt feels relieved. He turns now to the girl who's been sitting alone and asks her to join the group of four girls in order to make the group sizes more equal. She makes no move. Then he hears one of the four girls say, 'Oh. My. God. Not the Brontosaurus. Quick! Get the air freshener.' The others snigger and look sideways at Matt.

In two strides he is at their table, looming over them. 'I don't like bullies', he says. 'You got that? Zero tolerance. And I'm watching you now.'

'What?' says one of the girls, truculently. 'What you getting in *my* face for? I never said nothing. It was her.' She shoved her neighbour with her elbow. Her neighbour grinned and shoved her back.

'Just remember. Zero tolerance.' Matt turns on his heel and goes over to Bronte. She's staring at him like a rabbit in the headlights. When he tells her to go and join the adult group she looks relieved and takes her stuff over. As she moves ponderously across he notices that, even by today's standards, the poor kid is very overweight. He wonders whether he could be handling all this better.

He's just finished reminding everyone that they have five minutes left now to read carefully through the contract when Celia, one of the adult students, calls him over. He approaches her smiling, but she's looking distinctly grim. 'You're chastising the wrong group', she tells him, in a stage whisper that's probably audible all the way down the corridor.

'Sorry?' says Matt.

'The wrong group', she says again, pointing at the girls he's just told off. 'It's the other lot. *Them*.' And she points at the table where Hanni and her friends are sitting quietly, reading the handout. 'They're the bullies. Always sniggering and whispering. Just you ask these two.' She nods towards Bronte and Oliver who are now sitting opposite her at the same table. They both keep their heads down, clearly embarrassed. 'They do nothing but torment them', Celia went on. 'And it's time somebody did something about it. And let me tell you, they snigger at us, too. The three of us. All the time. Because we're old, apparently. And nobody picks them up on it. And what I want to know is: why doesn't anybody challenge them? Is it because you people are scared of being called racist?'

Matt holds up his hand. 'Okay, Celia. Listen. If I see that sort of behaviour I'll challenge it, okay? But I can't do anything about it unless I see it. I'll pass on what you've said to Alia…'

'But you're her boss, aren't you?'

'*No*. No, I'm not. Why ever would you think that?'

'Well...' Celia appears to consider the question. 'Because you're a man?'

Matt stares at her. Then he remembers to check his watch. Five minutes gone. He turns round and addresses the class. 'Okay. Everybody finished reading?'

'No', says Celia. 'Obviously I haven't. How could I get it read when you've been keeping me talking?'

Section C

Thirty-five minutes later Matt is taking the stairs down to the canteen. He thinks he managed to hold it together. He kept the class onside – just about. As far as he could ascertain without a formal test, the learning outcomes were met. But he feels as though he's been through a shredder. He needs to get clear in his head what he did right and what he got wrong and what to do now with what he knows about that class. How come Alia didn't give him the heads-up? Has she not noticed all those tensions and all that animosity running just below the surface? With her away today he's beginning to feel increasingly isolated.

Then, when he walks into the canteen, his mood lifts to see a familiar face. It's Jenni. She's sitting alone, wolfing a baguette, so he goes over to join her, slings his bag down under the table and sits himself on the spare chair. She looks a bit alarmed – or maybe that's just how anyone would look with a mouth full of French bread.

'Okay if I sit here?' he says, a bit belatedly.

'Fine', she says, which sends a spray of crumbs over him and over the table. He resists brushing himself down.

Jenni swallows and then smiles and asks him how things are going. He tells her about the class. Once he gets started it's like he can't stop. It all comes out, every detail. She's a good listener. She keeps her eyes on him. She nods. Every now and again she asks him a question. She doesn't look at her watch, even though he knows he's going on a bit. She's alright, is Jenni. 'The thing is', he says, finally, 'why didn't Alia warn me?'

Jenni thinks for a minute. 'You know what?' she says. 'It might be that none of this stuff has surfaced when she's been teaching them. Like, if she doesn't get them working in groups, for example – if she's taking a more teacher-centred approach – there'd be no opportunity for the cracks to show. But you're going to have to tell her, Matt. She needs to know. Everybody who teaches that group needs to know what's going on.'

'You're right', says Matt. 'The trouble is –'. The trouble is that he has to talk to Alia about the mess Mo's dropped him in, and what with this as well, it's going to be complete overload. She'll begin to wish she wasn't his mentor.

'What?' says Jenni. 'Matt, you can't not tell her. At least, you have to tell somebody. I mean, look what we're talking about here.' She ticks off on her fingers, 'Bullying. Ageism. Possibly racism...'

'And sexism', says Matt. 'Celia assumed I was Jenni's boss – just because I'm a bloke.'

'Well, the college has an anti-bullying policy, and a policy on inclusion and equality. All college policies are required to include clear guidance on how to report infringements, and who to. Have you got your laptop in there?' She nods towards his bag. 'Let's look them up. And then, if you don't want to bother Alia with it, you'll know who to report it to direct.'

'What about the two who sit on their own?' he says, while they watch the screen, waiting for his old laptop to wake up properly. 'What can be done about that? I mean, they may be better off out of the groups if it saves them being bullied. But we should be stopping the bullying, not allowing kids to sit alone just so we can avoid tackling the problem.'

'I think some people are just self-isolates', says Jenni. 'They prefer sitting alone, working alone. They don't want to be part of a group. And there's some who want to join in but aren't allowed to. The group excludes them. And it's not always easy to tell the difference. So you have to approach it carefully. The danger is you can end up forcing someone into a group who really does prefer working alone. Then you're just putting an obstacle between them and their learning.'

Matt pulls up the college website and finds the link to college policies. They scroll through the anti-bullying policy first. When they get to the section on procedures Matt puts his hands on his head in frustration. '*All incidents or suspected incidents of bullying should be reported immediately to the Assistant Principal, Head of Staff Development.* They've got to be kidding. That's Gail effing Clifford.'

'What's the problem?' says Jenni. 'You mean because she's a bit of a bully herself?'

'No. Well, yeah, she is, isn't she. But it's more complicated than that. Hang on.'

They scroll through the college policy on inclusion and equality. Matt closes the laptop with a bang. 'Same thing', he says. 'Report to the Space Invader.' He swears under his breath, then apologises.

Jenni is looking at him with concern. 'What's going on, Matt? There's something you're not telling me.'

He sighs and rubs his head. 'Long story', he says. 'Are you free after work? I'll buy you a beer.'

He's surprised to see her blush, from forehead to neck. 'Okay', she says. 'You're on.'

Part two: Critical thinking activities

The tasks in this part of the chapter encourage you to reflect on Matt's experiences and to make professional judgements about inclusion, diversity, the definitions of bullying and, above all, the principles of equality and social justice in the college and in your classroom.

These tasks also encourage you to consider how the situations and questions which Matt has encountered might relate to, or arise in, your own experience as a teacher. In working through these tasks you may find it useful to keep a reflective journal, make notes, or to engage in discussion with an experienced colleague or mentor.

Activity 1

In section A, Matt receives an unpleasant surprise when he discovers that Mo has made a complaint against him. The questions in this activity focus on issues of professionalism, organisational etiquette and communication. When formulating your answers, consider whether and to what extent these questions might apply in your own institution.

a) Matt is expecting his meeting with Gail Clifford to be about the envelope of money he found and handed in, but she has quite a different agenda, which comes as a shock to him. What the senior manager does here is to spring on him what is sometimes referred to as an *ambush agenda*. In your view, does this conform to reasonable expectations of professional management behaviour? Think carefully about the reasons for your answer.

b) Hopefully you have never experienced an *ambush* yourself over quite such a serious matter, but consider now whether you have ever found yourself in a position of meeting with a line manager without being clear beforehand what the meeting was about. How did this feel? Have you ever *ambushed* a colleague yourself in this way? To what extent might this be seen as a form of bullying?

c) Look again at how Matt behaved in this situation. How would you rate the professionalism of his response? Is there anything he could have done differently to improve the situation? How do you think you might have responded in this situation, and why?

d) In your view, is Mo justified in making a formal complaint against Matt? If so, why? And if you consider this course of action unjustified, what do you think are Mo's reasons for taking it?

Activity 2

This section shows us what happens when Matt covers Alia's class. It raises questions about professionalism, social justice and institutional policy, as well as about principles of teaching and learning. This activity provides the opportunity for you to reflect on all of these.

a) Matt forces himself not to dwell on the accusations made against him, but to put thoughts of that aside and concentrate on teaching the class. Do you think he makes the right decision here? Consider carefully the reasons for your answer.

b) Think back over your own experience as a teacher or trainee teacher. Has there ever been an occasion when a serious problem – at work or at home – has intruded on your teaching day? If so, how did you handle this, and why? With hindsight, would you have done anything differently?

c) Matt encounters a complex set of problems with this group. Identify at least four issues which urgently require addressing. How would you rank these in terms of priority, and why?

d) When Matt is introducing himself to the group, why do you think: (i) He tells them he's been looking forward to meeting them? (ii) He starts the introductions with the three adults? (iii) He addresses the man as *sir*?

e) Look again at how Matt handles the issue with Oliver. In your view, could he have handled this better, and if so, how? What are the advantages and disadvantages of his approach?

f) Look again at how Matt handles the issue with Bronte. Again, in your view, could he have handled this better, and if so, how? What does he do well here and what could he have done differently?

g) Consider different ways in which Matt could have handled Celia's request to speak to him. Did he need to listen to her straight away? What might have been (i) the advantages and (ii) the disadvantages of telling her they could have a chat at the end of the lesson?

h) What is your view of Matt's response to Celia's complaint? What would your own response have been, under these circumstances?

i) What further issues are raised by Celia's assumption that Matt is Alia's boss? This is the second time people have mistaken his status. What do you think is the underlying cause here?

Activity 3

Here we see Matt discussing the class with Jenni. Seeking and providing peer support are important aspects of being a professional. The questions in this activity focus both on the issues Matt raises and on what constitutes positive peer support.

a) Matt leaves the classroom needing to get it clear in his own mind 'what he did right and what he did wrong'. If he were to sound you out about this, what would you tell him, and why?

b) He finds that Jenni is *a good listener*. What is it specifically that he notices about the way she listens? Have you ever discussed your teaching with a colleague or mentor and found that they were *not* a good listener? If so, what were the signs? In your view, are you yourself a good listener when colleagues talk to you about their work?

c) Jenni suggests that perhaps it is Alia's choice of teaching and learning methods with this class that has made the problems of bullying and cliques less obvious to see. Think about your own most frequently used teaching strategies. Are these likely to help you see whether problems of this sort exist within a class?

d) Matt and Jenni diagnose a number of problems within the class, including attitudes of ageism and sexism. What evidence would you point to in order to support their diagnosis?

e) Matt and Jenni discuss the problem of isolates – learners who sit and work alone. Jenni suggests that this issue must be approached carefully, as the learner may simply be exercising a preference. In your view, how might a teacher best discover whether sitting alone is the learner's genuine choice, or the result of them being excluded and isolated by some or all of their classmates?

f) Are you familiar with your own college's policy or policies on anti-bullying and inclusion? Would you know whom to approach if you needed to report an incident of bullying or similar infringement? If not, take this opportunity to familiarise yourself with the policies, paying particular attention to (i) the definitions of bullying and (ii) the procedures and processes of reporting an incident.

And finally...

» *You will find some helpful texts relating to the topics covered in this story listed under Further Reading at the back of this book.*

» *To find out whether Matt is able to make his own case heard and to challenge the damage Mo is trying to do to his reputation with the college management, you'll need to read on...*

Story 6 Working with adult learners

Chapter aims

This story will help you to reflect on:

- the characteristics and needs of adult learners;

- how to recognise and address the problems faced by adult returners;

- the teacher–learner dynamic in the context of adult learning;

- teaching and learning strategies appropriate to adult learners;

- issues of teacher confidence and competence when working with adult learners;

- how to motivate and engage adult learners;

- how to develop strategies for dealing with difficult situations which arise when teaching adult learners.

Part one: Jenni and the grown-ups

Section A

Jenni was heading for her first afternoon class. It was an adult group on an Access to Higher Education course. To her surprise, the Terrible Tuesday class had been taken off her time-table after all, thanks to an intervention from her mentor, and she had been allocated this Access class to replace them. She was looking forward to meeting them. Teaching a group of well-motivated adults promised to be so much more civilized than struggling with a bunch of youngsters who didn't really want to be there. But it wasn't her adult class that was on her mind as she hurried down the corridor, brushing baguette crumbs from the front of her jacket. It was Matt. What had just happened? This drink they were going to have – was it just that, a friendly drink between colleagues? Yes, she told herself. Obviously. Just a colleague thing. He was probably married. And anyway, until this morning she hadn't really liked him very much. She'd thought he was a bit of a know-it-all. But just now he'd seemed quite – well – quite vulnerable, really. She knew she ought to be concentrating on the task in hand – going through the lesson plan one more time in her head. But her mind suddenly seemed to be all over the place.

She arrived at the classroom in good time and started shifting the tables about to create one large boardroom table arrangement, more appropriate, in her view, to adult learners than leaving the tables in rows. The effort left her feeling sweaty and a bit out of breath; but she was able to greet the learners with a smile as they arrived, fairly promptly, and surveyed the room.

'What's this?' said a burly, grey-haired man with a ponytail. 'This is a bit different, isn't it?'

'Where's the normal teacher?' demanded a twenty-something woman with a face full of piercings.

'Don't worry', joked Jenni. 'I'm fairly normal, too.'

It didn't get the laugh she expected. Of course, she thought. They'd just got used to one teacher and now the timetable had been changed so that she could take over. That was bound to unsettle them. So she explained that she was their new teacher and that she was looking forward to getting to know them and working with them this term. 'But first things first', she said. 'Let's do introductions. I'm Jenni. And I've got this beanbag here. I'm going to throw it to you one at a time and when you catch the beanbag I want you to introduce yourself and then throw it back to me. Okay?'

'Why don't we just introduce ourselves?' asked Ponytail. 'And skip the beanbag? It'd save time.'

'I think you'll enjoy it more this way', said Jenni in her jolliest voice. 'Okay. Catch.'

Ponytail's name, it turned out, was Dave. The woman with a face full of studs and rings was Lucy. They each caught the beanbag, announced their name and threw it back. If they were enjoying it, it didn't show. Jenni chucked it next at an older woman in sensible shoes and a waxed jacket. It hit her in the face.

'Whoops', said Jenni. 'Sorry. Are you alright?'

'No', said the woman. 'I've probably sustained a bruise. My name is Mrs Lambert. And I'd like to suggest that we dispense with this silly game, introduce ourselves like normal human beings and get on with what we came here to do – which is to learn.'

There were murmurs of agreement all round. Jenni, noticing for the first time that one of the learners had his arm in a sling, decided that her best course of action was to back down before she broke someone's nose.

She switched on the data projector and began her lesson introduction. She explained the learning objectives and the shape the lesson was going to take. She put a lot of energy and enthusiasm into her voice – a valuable strategy she'd learnt from her mentor – and she offered lots of positive eye contact to the learners, all twelve of them, who were now seated around the table. One, however, wasn't meeting her eye. In fact, he was reading a newspaper.

He was holding it open in front of him so that he was completely hidden behind it. Unable to see his face, Jenni had to work out by a process of elimination that this was a man who had introduced himself as Bob.

'Er, Bob?' she said. 'Are we ready?'

The newspaper didn't shift. 'You might be', was the response from behind it. 'But I'm not – quite.'

'It must be an interesting article', she said, brightly. 'Do you want to tell us what it's about?' She could see the eyes of the class moving from her to Bob and back again as though watching a tennis match.

Bob rattled his paper but didn't lower it. 'It's about teachers being overpaid', he said.

Some of the class chuckled at this, and then all eyes moved to Jenni, waiting to see what she would do.

'Well, at the moment, Bob, I'm being paid to do nothing. But whose fault is that?'

There was a collective intake of breath and all eyes moved to Bob. He lowered the paper slowly and smiled at her. '*Touché*', he said.

Relieved, Jenni resumed the planned lesson. 'I'm going to talk through this topic for about ten minutes', she said. 'I'll be putting the slides up afterwards on the college net, but you might like to take notes as well. I always find it helps me to remember stuff if I do that. And it's good practice if you're planning to go into higher education. Stop me if I go too fast or if you need any clarification. Otherwise, I'll take questions at the end of this bit.'

Mrs Lambert raised her hand. 'Could I just ask a question before we get started?' she said. And, without waiting for a nod, went on, 'Why are we all having to sit around this table? Why can't we sit as we usually do, in rows? We look as if we're children at a birthday party. If I want to look at you or at the screen I have to turn my head sideways all the time and with my arthritis that's rather painful for me.'

Jenni explained the advantages of a boardroom seating arrangement; the ease with which eye contact could be made with everyone else in the class, facilitating discussion and interaction; the move away from the sort of schoolroom model which might have negative associations for some adults returning to education; the removal of the barrier between teacher and learners.

'That's all very well', said Mrs Lambert, 'but as far as I'm concerned it's a pain in the neck.'

There were some chuckles. Again, Jenni was aware of the class's watchfulness, the tennis match shifts of gaze. She suggested that Mrs Lambert swap places with someone so that she could sit facing directly front. Ponytail Dave at once offered his seat, and the exchange was made. Jenni checked her watch, already fifteen minutes into the lesson time and she hadn't really got started yet. She was going to have to think quickly and make some adjustments to her lesson plan, but not yet. She had to lay the foundations first with this initial bit of exposition. Then perhaps she'd trim down some of the discussion – conduct it as a whole group rather than in pairs as planned. That way, there'd be no need for the whole group debrief.

The ten-minute exposition with PowerPoint slides went smoothly. There were no interruptions. Everyone was taking notes of one kind or another – Mr Arm-in-a-sling was recording it all on his phone – and she seemed to have got the pace about right. When she'd finished she invited questions and comments.

Lucy, with the face piercings, put up her hand. 'Is that thing off now?' she said, nodding towards Arm-in-a-sling's phone. 'I don't want to be recorded asking some thick question. He ought to have asked our permission to have that on. I don't know about anybody else, but I don't want to ask anything or say anything if it's being recorded. There was things I wanted to ask you just now, but I couldn't, because he'd got that thing on.' She glared at Arm-in-a-sling. He shrugged, looked embarrassed and put his phone away. 'We should have been asked', she said, making her point again to no one in particular.

'Yes, you're right; I should have asked whether you were all comfortable with it', said Jenni. 'It's my fault, not his. Don't be cross with him. Tell you what, can I have a volunteer who'll give him a copy of their notes until his arm's better? Someone who's taken electronic notes or someone with nice clear handwriting?'

Several volunteers raised their hands, and Jenni thanked them and asked them to sort that out after the lesson. 'What happened to your arm, by the way?' she asked.

'Had it twisted to come on this course', he said.

Jenni laughed. 'Well, I hope it'll turn out to be worth it', she said.

There were a few chuckles at that. 'Okay', she said quickly. 'Let's get back on track. Any other questions or comments?'

Ponytail Dave raised his hand. 'I think you got your dates wrong', he said. 'I think you'll find that the Equality Act of 2010 covers cases of discrimination that take place from October of that year, not before.'

Jenni felt the blood rush to her face. Her worst nightmare about teaching an adult class had been that they'd know more than she did. 'Are you sure?' she asked, as calmly as she could.

Dave tapped at his tablet and then held it up. She walked round to look at it. She read the Gov UK page quickly. He was right. This was terrible! She could feel herself panicking. What to do?

Then, 'Thank you so much, Dave', she heard herself saying. 'You're absolutely right. And I'm very grateful that you spotted that. I'm sure we all are. So what that means, of course, everybody, is that any incident occurring before October 2010 has to be dealt with under the old legislation, even if the case is brought to court after the new legislation replaced it. Tell us how you spotted that, Dave. What's your expertise here?'

'No expertise, really', said Dave. He's blushing himself now. 'I ended up having to take an employer to court for age discrimination, that's all. So I had to familiarise myself with all this stuff.'

'Did you win?' asked Newspaper Bob.

'Aye, I did. And that's what's paying my fees from here all the way until I get a degree.'

Jenni began clapping her hands together in applause and gradually the rest of the class joined in. Dave beamed.

'This is one of the great things about teaching a class of adults,' Jenni told them. 'There's so much experience and expertise to share – it often turns out to be a learning experience for the teacher, too.'

Section B

On the whole, when it was all over, Jenni felt she'd survived the lesson fairly well. But it certainly hadn't been the easy ride she'd expected. It would have been really useful to talk it all over with someone – the good bits and the difficult bits – but she was reluctant to try her mentor, Eleni, again and only end up with the latest bulletin on Nic-with-a-C. She hadn't got time for that. She had two more classes to teach this afternoon. And afterwards she was going for that drink with Matt. The best thing, she decided, was to drop Eleni an email. If she checked her work emails as often as she checked her personal ones there should be a fairly quick response. So, dashing to her desk in the shared office, Jenni roused her computer out of its hibernation mode and wrote:

> *Hi Eleni*
>
> *Just taught the Access to HE group. My first time with an adult class. Not as easy as I thought it would be! Should have asked for a few tips from you first. What's your advice for next time?*
>
> *Jenni*

She hit send, scooped up her handouts and lesson plan, and set off at a run for her next class.

By the end of the afternoon she felt exhausted. Her last two classes had gone well, but she was conscious that her energy was flagging and that for the last hour or so she wasn't injecting quite her usual level of enthusiasm and fun into her teaching. Handling that adult class had taken more out of her than she had realised. Back in the office she sat down heavily at her desk and nudged the computer screen into life. There it was already: a reply from Eleni. She opened it up. It was a long email. Keeping her fingers crossed that it wasn't going to be a lengthy lament about Nic, Jenni leaned forward and began reading.

Hi Jenni

Hope it wasn't too bad. You obviously survived! But yes, there are some important things to keep in mind about adult learners – characteristics and needs that are different from those of 16–19-year-olds. I'll bullet point them for you:

- *First of all, a lot of them are what we call <u>adult returners</u> – people who are returning to education after a long break. Maybe they've been out of education since they left school at 16. This means that their expectations and levels of confidence have been shaped by their early experience of school. They may feel ill-prepared and scared of appearing stupid. They may think everybody else knows stuff they don't. And they may assume that learning is going to be painful or boring or incredibly difficult. So they need gentle handling and a lot of reassurance.*

- *On the other hand, adult learners bring loads of life experience and work expertise to a class. This makes them a really valuable resource and it's important to make sure you draw on this as much as possible.*

- *Adult learners usually have a lot of other commitments – family, jobs, social responsibilities. This means their time is precious to them. They need to feel their time in college is being spent productively. Keeping up the pace in lessons is important.*

- *As well as investing their time, they are often investing their own money in attending college. They have to feel they're getting their money's worth. Lessons need to be packed with plenty of substance. You need to select methods that are time-effective as well as adult-appropriate. For example, they may prefer to be told information rather than be sent away to find it out for themselves.*

- *They may have childcare or other responsibilities so you need to be flexible over matters of punctuality and finish times.*

- *You need to establish a relationship with them that is conducted in an adult-to-adult way, where you are all working towards the same goal: their success on the course. If you make a mistake, admit it. If there's something you don't know, tell them. (Personally, I think this applies just as much with classes of younger learners.) Above all, avoid appearing patronising.*

- *But don't forget – just because we can talk about 'the characteristics of adult learners', this doesn't mean that all adult learners are somehow the same. There'll be just as many differences in levels of confidence, enthusiasm, engagement, note-taking skills and ability to problem-solve as you'll find in any class of 16–19-year-olds. So never make the mistake of lumping them all together or not taking individual needs and idiosyncrasies into account.*

- *And finally, NEVER over-estimate their confidence. They are likely to be much more nervous about being in the classroom situation than you are!*

Come over and have a chat soon. Tell me how it went.

Best wishes,

Eleni

It was obvious that Eleni had taken a lot of time and effort to put together this reply. It made Jenni feel a bit guilty. Perhaps she should spend more time being grateful for Eleni's strengths as a mentor from now on, instead of dwelling on the woman's ridiculous boyfriend fixation. She read through the email again. It was a useful list. Okay, so most of it came down to common sense. But there were certainly a couple of things in there that – had she thought about them beforehand – would have saved her some grief this afternoon.

Section C

She was meeting Matt at 6pm, so there wasn't time to go home and change – which was probably a good thing because she wouldn't have been able to decide what to wear. This way there was no choice. So she sat at her desk and caught up on some marking before packing up and crossing the road to the Witch and Hound. Matt was already in there, sitting behind a pint. She got one for herself and joined him. There weren't many people in yet, just a group of students on the far side of the bar and two old men at the next table playing dominoes.

'So how was your day?' asked Matt.

Grateful for someone to discuss it with, she launched into an account of the afternoon's adult class. Some of it seemed quite funny to her now in the telling – even if it hadn't at the time. They both laughed about the beanbag game, and when she came to the bit about Bob and his newspaper Matt said, 'Well, at least you didn't go over and set fire to it.'

'Thing is, I didn't take time to get to know them properly', she said. 'Knowing their names – that's important – but it's not enough somehow. If I was doing it again I think I'd ask them to introduce each other and tell me why they'd decided at this point to re-enter education and aim for HE. That way I wouldn't be teaching blind, you know?'

'Sounds like you turned it all around in the end', said Matt. 'Something I've come to realise over the past few weeks: teaching – it's all about winning hearts and minds, yeah?'

Jenni nodded. 'Oh, but we didn't come here to talk about me', she said brightly. 'So come on then. Your turn. Spill the beans.'

He leaned forward. 'Okay. But let's keep the sound down', he said in a voice only just above a whisper.

'Oh. Right.' She leaned forward, too. She was willing to play along up to a point, as long as this wasn't about him being married and out on the sly.

'I went to see Gail Clifford this morning', he said quietly. 'I wanted to ask her about something – I'll tell you what in a minute. That's another story. But who do I see coming out of her office but Mo. You know Mo, from Health and Social Care?'

'Sort of.'

'Well, he comes out smirking all over his face. Turns out he'd been in there and made a complaint against me. Told her I'd been unprofessional and caused trouble with his learners. So she's given me a formal warning. Unless Alia sets the record straight when she gets back tomorrow, I'm out on my ear. No more teaching placement. And if the accusation sticks, I'll be off the teacher training course. Bye bye, new career.'

'And did you?' asked Jenni.

'Did I what?'

'Cause trouble with his learners?'

'No', said Matt. 'Well, not intentionally. They don't like him. They were hoping I was his replacement. But that's his doing, not mine.'

'But Alia can vouch for you, can't she?' asked Jenni. 'Did she see everything?'

'She observed me take one lesson', said Matt. 'But there were some conversations between me and Mo when she wasn't there, obviously.'

Jenni bit her lip.

'You don't fancy my chances, do you?' said Matt. She'd not seen him like this before, drawn with worry. He'd always looked so confident, as though nothing could touch him.

'It'll be your word against his', she said. 'But Alia'll be able to vouch for the way you've always, to her knowledge, conducted yourself in a professional manner. And I'll speak up for you, too, if necessary. I can tell Gail Clifford how professionally you behaved when you sat in on my classes. We'll back you. Don't give up.'

Matt raised his glass to her. 'You're a star', he said.

To cover her embarrassment, Jenni said, 'So, you were going to tell me why you went to Clifford's office.'

'Yeah, well. This is where it gets really weird. I found an envelope full of cash under a table in room 108. I took it over and handed it in to Clifford and I've never heard another word. Not from her. Not from the police. Nothing.'

'You're kidding me! Well, maybe she kept it', said Jenni, and grinned.

But Matt obviously didn't find it funny. 'One thing's for sure', he said, 'someone's decided to keep it quiet. And what I want to know is why.'

Part two: Critical thinking activities

The tasks in this part of the chapter encourage you to think about the pleasures and the difficulties of teaching adult learners. If you already have experience of teaching this age group you will be able to draw on your existing knowledge and compare your approach and ideas to Jenni's. If you have yet to teach an adult class you can draw on your own experiences as an adult learner to evaluate and reflect on some of the issues discussed here.

Activity 1

The questions in this section focus on Jenni's experience with the adult class she had been looking forward so much to teaching. You may find it useful to read section A through again carefully before considering your answers.

a) Heading for the class, Jenni tells herself that 'teaching a group of well-motivated adults promised to be so much more civilized than struggling with a bunch of youngsters who didn't really want to be there.' On what do you suppose she bases this assumption? Have you ever made this same assumption yourself? In your own experience – either as a teacher or as an adult learner – how have you found adult learners' motivation compares with that of 16–19-year-olds? What examples can you cite to support your answer?

b) We only hear about the first half hour or so of the lesson, but there is a lot going on during that time. If you were helping Jenni to evaluate her teaching skills based on this, what would you identify as her strengths and what would you suggest are areas for development? What examples would you cite to support your view?

c) What do you think Jenni hoped to achieve by introducing the beanbag name game? She decides to abandon it. Do you think this was a good decision? What reasons would you give to support your answer? Have you ever been in a similar situation where you have had to re-evaluate the usefulness of an activity or teaching method on the spot?

d) How well do think Jenni handled the incident with Bob and his newspaper? Would you have done anything differently? If so, what, and why?

e) In your view, how well does Jenni handle Mrs Lambert's objection to the table layout? Jenni explains why she considers the one large boardroom table a more appropriate seating arrangement for adults than leaving the tables in rows, but can you think of any advantages that she doesn't mention?

f) Lucy argues that learners should be asked their permission before any part of a lesson is recorded. Do you agree? What reasons would you give to support your answer?

g) How would you evaluate Jenni's handling of this incident? What would you yourself have done in this situation, and why?

h) How would you evaluate the way Jenni responds to the situation where the learner, Dave, points out her mistake? Is there anything she could or should have done differently?

i) Have you ever experienced a similar situation, as a teacher, learner or observer? If so, how was it handled, and what did you learn from the incident?

Activity 2

In this section, Jenni receives some helpful advice from her mentor, Eleni. The questions in this task relate to that advice and to how it might apply both to Jenni's class and to your own experience of (or hopes and anxieties about) teaching adult learners.

a)   Jenni feels that she has 'survived the lesson fairly well'. Based on the part of the lesson that we saw, do you agree? What evidence would you give to support your answer? In your view, is *surviving* a lesson a legitimate professional concern, and, if so, why?

b)   You will already have formed your own view about Eleni's strengths and weaknesses as a mentor. Does this section cause you to change your view, and, if so, in what way and why?

c)   Jenni observes that many of the points on Eleni's list are simply *common sense*. Thinking back to the account of her lesson, which of these points do you think she was already aware of and was able to act on at the time?

d)   Drawing on your own observations or experience – either as a teacher or an adult learner – suggest one more useful bullet point that Eleni could have added to the list of characteristics she emails to Jenni.

e)   What do you think are the *couple of things* in Eleni's list that Jenni finds particularly enlightening and relevant to the difficulties she experienced with her adult class?

Activity 3

In section C, Jenni and Matt tell each other about their recent difficulties. Some of the questions in this activity require you to think back to earlier events in Chapters 2 and 3, while others encourage you to reflect on your understanding of professionalism and teacher–student interactions.

a)   Jenni expresses the view that, *'Knowing [learners'] names – that's important – but it's not enough.'* To what extent do you agree with what she is saying here? What do you suppose she believes are the advantages of getting to know something about each individual adult learner?

b)   The additional information that Jenni believes would have been useful is to do with why each learner has decided to re-enter education and aim for HE. How would this knowledge help her in planning their lessons and supporting their learning?

c)   In your own experience, either as a teacher of adults or as an adult learner, how usual is it for teachers to take the time to ask this sort of question?

d)   Matt declares that successful teaching is '*all about winning hearts and minds*'. What do you think he means by this? Do you think this applies any more to the teaching of adult learners than to younger ones?

e)   When Matt recounts to Jenni what happened to him that morning – including his description of Mo coming out '*smirking all over his face*', does he, in your view, keep within acceptable parameters of professional behaviour? Make sure you can give clear reasons to support your answer.

f)   Matt claims that Mo's learners' preference for him is Mo's own fault. Do you agree? Have you ever been in a similar position to Matt's, where learners have told you that they prefer you to their regular teacher? If so, how did you handle the situation? If not, how would you handle it if it arose?

g)   Jenni says she will vouch for Matt's professional behaviour when he sat in on her class. And yet we know, from Chapter 2, that she found having him there quite difficult at the time. Looking back at Chapters 2 and 3, do you see any similarities between the way Matt behaved in Jenni's class and the way he behaved in Mo's? To what extent do you think it was the *mindset* of Jenni and Mo that was different, rather than Matt's behaviour?

And finally...

»   *You will find some helpful texts relating to the topics covered in this story, including the concept of* mindset, *listed under Further Reading at the back of this book.*

»   *To find out whether or not Jenni succeeds in putting some of Eleni's advice into practice with her adult class, and whether Alia is able or willing to rescue Matt, you'll need to read on...*

Story 7 Being a subject specialist

Chapter aims

This story will help you to reflect on:

- what is required of a subject specialist within your vocational area;

- your responsibility, as a subject specialist, to keep updated and/or upskilled in your own field;

- the range of ways in which you can achieve this;

- the relationship between subject specialism and choice of teaching/learning methods;

- ways to use learner experience and expertise as a resource when teaching at higher levels;

- teaching and learning strategies appropriate to higher levels of qualification;

- issues of teacher confidence and competence when teaching higher level qualifications;

- how to develop strategies for dealing with potential difficulties arising from teaching higher level qualifications.

Part one: Alia and the higher level learners

Section A

Alia had enjoyed the previous day's conference at the local university. It had been all about teaching higher education courses in further education college. She was due to teach her first session on the foundation degree today, so the timing couldn't have been better. She had to admit that the prospect of teaching at this level had been making her feel nervous. Apart from doing the odd guest spot on the in-house teacher training course, this would be the first time she taught above level 3. But the conference, which had involved lots of useful workshops and discussions, had got her all fired up; she'd gone home last night and entirely re-planned her lesson.

The conference had stressed the need to challenge level 4 learners and to encourage them to think critically and analytically. Alia was pretty sure she did this with all her learners, whatever the level; but with this group she was meeting today, a key aim would be to equip them with the skills and motivation they would need to become independent learners, able to pursue their own lines of research and construct well-reasoned arguments. It was scary, yes, but exciting to be doing something new and facing a new challenge. She remembered how she had felt just like this when, after a year of teaching level 2, she'd been given some level 3 classes on her timetable. That was only three years ago, but it seemed much longer. It was as though she'd been a different person then – only recently qualified and still not confident in her own strengths. Now here she was – a mentor and a level 4 tutor. If someone had told her back then how far she would come in just three years she'd never have believed them.

As she headed for the entrance of the bright red Pillarbox building she congratulated herself on how well she had prepared and researched the subject for this class. She had read carefully around her topic, both in the press and in a couple of professional journals she'd been able to access electronically. So she was confident that all the factual content of her lesson would be current and accurate. She'd also spent some time putting together a pretty impressive PowerPoint presentation with animated slides, sound effects and a couple of links to short clips on YouTube. She wanted to be sure of holding their attention because she was planning to talk for longer than she would to a level 2 or 3 class – not a lecture exactly, but a long enough bit of exposition to give them a sense of what it was like to attend an HE lecture. The other thing she'd done to prepare herself was to check with Learner Support whether there were any individuals in the group with specific learning needs that she would have to take into account when planning and conducting the lesson. Apparently there were not.

As she climbed the stairs she found that, despite all this careful preparation, she was beginning to feel a bit nervous. She told herself that this was a good thing. She could remember from four years ago her teacher training tutor saying to her that the day you don't feel nervous before a class is the day you ought to give up teaching. He'd said that nerves, or the adrenalin, or whatever you wanted to call it, meant that you were psyching yourself up to do a good job, that you were bothered. Well, she was certainly beginning to feel bothered now! Would the class like her? Would they ask questions she couldn't answer? Had she pitched the lesson at the right level? Would they find it patronisingly easy? Or punishingly difficult? Had she included enough material in her plan to last the lesson?

Stop it! She told herself. *You're an experienced and competent teacher. Whatever this morning throws at you, you're going to be able to handle it.*

And, right on cue, she was thrown something she certainly hadn't been expecting: Matt, looking uncharacteristically anxious, striding quickly towards her down the corridor and grabbing her arm.

'Alia! Thank goodness! I need your help.'

'Nice to see you, too', she said, looking pointedly at his hand until he let go of her.

'Sorry', he said. 'Really sorry. But I'm in deep sh– I'm in trouble, Alia. Mo's persuaded Gail Clifford I've turned his students against him. I need you to go and tell her the truth, that I've not been unprofessional.'

'Matt, I'm on my way to teach', she said. 'I can't go and see anybody right now. Tell me about it later, okay?' She edged past him and carried on towards the classroom.

He called after her: 'But will you speak up for me?'

'Ask me later', she said over her shoulder. Adding to herself, *Because teaching comes first.*

Section B

It was a very small class in comparison to those she was used to. And, presumably because it represented the college's highest level of provision, it was accommodated in one of a shiny new suite of rooms at the top of the Pillarbox building, with interactive whiteboard, two different data projectors and a console with a whole bank of buttons and switches – all unlabelled – which doubled as a lectern with microphone, the sort from behind which American presidents made their speeches. Taking up position behind it, Alia worried she must look a bit like Davros, leader of the Daleks. 'Oh dear', she said to the small group facing her, her voice booming through the microphone. 'I feel as though I'm about to give a State of the Nation address.'

No one laughed.

This won't do, she thought. I can't stand behind that. She peered at the rows of buttons, wondering which one would activate the data projector. There were no clues. The hand in which she was grasping the data stick containing her PowerPoint was growing sweaty. She pressed a button and the room lights were extinguished. Having no windows, the room was immediately plunged into complete darkness. There was a collective gasp from the class. Quickly she pushed what she thought was the same button again. No lights, but the data projector purred into life.

'Use your phone to see by', advised a woman's voice from out of the darkness. 'Use the light from your phone.'

'I'm a claustrophobe', squeaked another voice – a man's – on the edge of panic. 'Please. I don't like this. I've got to get out.'

There was some shuffling and grunting and someone gave a loud, 'Ouch!' Alia had taken her phone from her pocket and was shining it at the console. Which button had she pressed to start with? Ah! This one! She jabbed it and the room was flooded with light. Eight of the nine students were squinting at her, dazzled. The ninth – a heavily built man in a fur-hooded anorak – was halfway to the door, paused in mid-escape like a prisoner in a spotlight.

'Sorry!' said Alia to the class at large. 'That's not got us off to a very good start, has it?' And then, to the man in the anorak, 'Would you still like to go out for some fresh air? Or are you okay to sit down now?'

'Depends whether you're going to switch the lights out again', he said.

Alia laughed. 'I promise you I'm not', she said. 'And I'm going to prop this door open – just in case none of you trust me on that.'

One or two of the learners laughed with her. Others were smiling good naturedly. She breathed a quiet sigh of relief. 'I'm Alia', she said. 'And I'm delighted to meet you all. I've been looking forward to working with you today. I'm a literacy and communications specialist. And, of course, that's a subject that's relevant right across the FE curriculum. So I get to teach people from a variety of vocational areas – which is really nice. You're all doing the foundation degree in Working with Young People, yes?'

There were murmurs of assent. Someone – she didn't quite see who – said, 'So they tell us', in a rather sarcastic tone.

'And one of the things you're going to be doing quite a lot of over the next year', Alia continued brightly, 'is to research and write assignments. And that's what I'm here to help you with. We're going to have a look this morning at some examples of writing and analyse what's good and not so good about them, and what their style tells us about their intended readership.'

A middle-aged woman on the front row raised her hand. She was wearing a bright red sweater with what looked like *Babe* knitted in white across her ample bosom. 'Can I just ask', she said, 'when we're going to actually *start* this degree? I mean, we've had inductions and introductions and orientations and library familiarisations. And now apparently you're going to tell us how to write our coursework. But what are we going to write coursework *about* if we're not being taught anything?'

'I can see you're keen to get started', said Alia. 'That's brilliant. And –'

'But my enthusiasm's fading fast', said the woman. She looked around her. 'I don't know about anyone else.'

'I'll certainly pass the message on', said Alia quickly. 'What's your name?'

The woman pointed to own chest. 'Babs', she said. 'I dunno how you could miss it.'

Alia found herself smiling at her own mistake. It would teach her to keep her glasses on. She looked around the class and saw that most of the learners were looking a bit more relaxed now, and some were smiling back at her. 'Okay', she said. 'Well, I was going to ask you each to introduce your neighbour to start off with. But I can see that you've probably had enough of all that and you're keen to get straight on with things. So can I just ask you to write your names on a piece of folded paper and prop it up in front of you – and then we can dive straight in.'

Section C

Alia began to feel more comfortable and confident as the lesson progressed. The first part of the PowerPoint slide show was all about the structure and presentation of a good assignment. The class laughed right on cue at the various cartoons and other visual jokes she'd included to illustrate the key points. Wearing her glasses now, she could see all their names clearly, and made sure she used them when asking and answering questions. Babs seemed to have cheered up a bit, and the learner who had experienced claustrophobia – and who had written his name in very small script: Tim – now appeared much more relaxed. And so, having lost a bit of time at the beginning of the lesson, Alia decided to carry straight on with her input rather than break things up with small group discussion as she had planned. After all, she thought, these were learners on an HE course and therefore should be able to cope with being lectured for a little while longer.

'You'll need to take a few notes during this next bit', she said. 'We're going to look at some pieces of writing and discuss their register and tone. Now, what about this one?' She clicked to the next slide. 'Take a couple of minutes to read it through. Oh, and you may want to comment on the punctuation, too – especially the use of semi-colons.'

She checked her watch. Two minutes should be plenty of time for them to read the page that was on the slide. It was copied from an actual assignment, though she'd taken great care to make sure the writer couldn't be identified. She noticed that some of the learners were discussing it with each other. Good. She checked her watch again.

'Okay, folks', she said. 'Time's up. What do we think? Who'd like to start us off? Tim?'

Tim looked awkward. 'This is probably a stupid question', he said. 'But what do you mean by 'register and tone'?'

It was immediately apparent that his question came as a huge relief to the other learners. They nodded and looked enquiringly at Alia.

She felt such a fool. This was a beginner's mistake. She could feel herself blushing, and she took off her glasses and polished them on her silk scarf to disguise her embarrassment. 'I'm so sorry', she said. 'Let's go back a step. I've used some unfamiliar terminology. No reason why you should be familiar with it. But it's going to be useful to you, so let me explain it.'

They listened attentively, took notes and asked one or two questions. She was just about to get back to discussing the slide when Babs raised her hand.

'While we're at it', she said, 'just tell us about semi-colons. Because I don't know about everybody else, but I've not got the foggiest idea about them. I can probably tell you what one is – and that's about it.' Again, there were nods of agreement and looks of relief all round. Alia, mortified, found herself polishing her glasses again.

Later, writing in her reflective journal as she ate her sandwich, Alia considered carefully what she'd learnt from her experience with the foundation degree class.

I made some really silly mistakes, she wrote; *the sort of mistakes an absolute beginner would make. I thought I'd prepared so carefully – and in some ways I had. And it all ended well. I liked them and they ended up liking me (I think), and I'll look forward to my next session with them. But that's only because I'm experienced enough – thank goodness – to spot what I did wrong.*

- *When I was planning I didn't take into account that they'd be impatient to get learning and that they'd already had plenty of time to get to know one another, especially as they are such a small group. So an 'introduction' activity would be mainly for my benefit and would seem a waste of time to them. I spotted that one in time, thank goodness.*

- *I made the classic mistake of a subject specialist – which was to use the jargon of my subject without thinking through whether they would be familiar with the meaning of the terms I was using. In future I must remember to introduce and define all terminology clearly.*

- *I assumed that, as students aiming at a degree, they would have a confident grasp of punctuation. Again, I think this was partly because punctuation's an aspect of my own subject and so I tend to over-estimate other adults' familiarity and confidence with it. But it was also about me making assumptions about what the students already knew, instead of creating activities within the lesson that allow me to find that out.*

- *And I should have gone up to have a look at that room and all its technical wizardry well before I had to teach in there. Then it wouldn't have come as such a shock to be faced with an array that looked like a control panel from the Tardis.*

She was just about to add a further bullet point when Jenni burst into her office.

Section D

'Quick!' said Jenni. 'I've got us an appointment with Gail Clifford. But we've got to go *now*.' She was red in the face and clearly very agitated.

Alia stared at her.

'It's about Matt', said Jenni, as though Alia ought to know this. 'Come *on*. Please?'

When they got to Gail Clifford's office the red STOP light was on above her door. Jenni knocked anyway and then walked in. 'We're your twelve o'clock appointment', she announced. 'And we can't hang about because we've both got classes to go to.'

Alia followed her in, admiring her nerve.

Gail Clifford, Assistant Principal in charge of staff development, looked up startled from her desk. The sound they heard when she opened her mouth was rather peculiar, like a high-pitched bark. Her two visitors glanced at one another in consternation. Was this an angry noise? Or was it just her lunch repeating?

It was neither, they realised, when a small dog trotted out from behind the desk, planted its forepaws and growled at them nastily.

'No! Bad boy!' snapped Clifford. 'Basket! Now!'

The dog retreated behind the desk, tail drooping.

As though nothing had happened, its owner demanded in roughly the same tone she'd used for the dog, 'So, Jenni, your first year in teaching. How's it going so far?'

'Fine, thanks', said Jenni. 'But –'

'And Alia', continued Clifford. 'How was the HE conference yesterday? Useful, I hope?'

'Very', said Alia. 'But that's not –'

'It's about Matt', said Jenni. 'Alia's come to tell you what really happened.' And she stepped aside, leaving Alia the floor.

'Look', said Alia, 'I don't know what's been said, or what accusations have been made, but I can vouch for the fact that Matt has behaved in an entirely professional way in every inter- action I've witnessed, whether it's with learners or with colleagues. His attitude towards the job is exemplary. He's going to be an excellent teacher. If some of Mo's learners have enjoyed having him teach them more than they've enjoyed having Mo, that's really not his fault.'

'Were you there when he threatened Mo?' asked Gail Clifford, coldly.

'*Threatened* him?'

'That's what Mo says.'

'Well that's rubbish', interrupted Jenni. 'Why would he do that? It's Mo that's been handing out the threats – how he's going to get him thrown out and stuff.'

'Were *you* there?' asked Clifford, turning her gaze on Jenni now.

'No, but –'

The Assistant Principal regarded them both for a moment. 'I'll have another word with Mo', she said. 'I'll tell him that you two have a different version of events. Oh, and Jenni, I think you ought to know that Mo's the colleague who'll be observing you for your annual peer assess- ment next week.'

Part two: Critical thinking activities

The following tasks encourage you to reflect on three key issues. One of these is your respon- sibilities as a subject specialist in your vocational field and how this shapes the way you pre- pare for your teaching. Another is how the level of qualification at which you are teaching may be reflected in your choice of teaching methods and your expectations of learners. And the third issue is about how you deal with the internal politics and professional conflicts which you may encounter within a large institution such as a college. If you already have experience of teaching higher level groups you will be able to draw on your existing knowledge and compare your approach and ideas to Alia's. If you have not, you can draw on your own experiences as a higher level learner on your teacher training programme to evaluate and reflect on some of the issues discussed here.

Activity 1

In this first section of the story, we find Alia preparing to teach a class at a higher level than she has taught before. For her it is a level 4 foundation degree class; however, anyone faced with teaching at a level above that which they are used to is likely to have similar concerns. When reflecting on your answers to the questions in this task, you may find it helpful to think of a time when you have been faced with teaching an unfamiliar class or topic at a level you have not taught before.

a) Alia is sure that she encourages all her learners, at whatever level, to think *critically and analytically*. What do you think this means in practice? In your view, how consistent is a critical or analytical approach with vocational competence-based learning?

b) Alia reflects on the ways she has prepared for this class. In your view, do her preparations differ in any way from how you might prepare for teaching learners at a lower level, such as level 2 for example? If so, how?

c) Think back to a time when you were preparing to teach a level of qualification for the first time. Identify one thing you did by way of preparation that Alia does not do. Or, alternatively, one thing you wish you had done in retrospect.

d) One of her preparatory actions is to contact Learner Support to check whether the class will include anyone with identified support needs. In your view, is this something specifically relevant to a higher level class? Why do you think she takes this action in this instance? Is this something you would do in the ordinary course of your planning? Give reasons to justify your answer.

e) What is your view of the advice Alia recalls from her teacher training tutor? Does it surprise you that Alia, an experienced teacher, is feeling nervous as the time for the lesson approaches? Do you yourself feel anxious to some degree before teaching a class? Are there some classes that make you feel more anxious than others? If so, what is it about those classes that causes the heightened anxiety? What action, if any, could you take to address this?

f) Alia lists the concerns she is feeling as she heads for the classroom. Which of these concerns do you recognise from when you yourself have been about to face a new class? Why do you think they are particularly relevant to Alia under her present circumstances?

g) Consider carefully the interaction in this section between Alia and Matt. Does anything here change your view of her as a mentor? Whom do you sympathise with most in this exchange: Alia or Matt – and why?

h) Alia's final words in this section are:'*Teaching comes first.*' In terms of priorities, is she right here, do you think? And if so, why?

Activity 2

In this second section of the story, we see that Alia's lesson gets off to rather a disastrous start. As you answer the following questions you might find it useful to consider whether the fact that Alia is an experienced and qualified teacher becomes evident at any point in the way she handles the various situations she encounters.

a) Alia's first difficulty arises from unfamiliar equipment and technology. Reflecting on your own experience of teaching (or of observing a lesson), what would you say are (i) the advantages and (ii) the disadvantages of reliance on technology for supporting teaching and learning?

b) In your view, could Alia have avoided this difficult start to the lesson, and if so, how? If you had been in Alia's position, what would you have learnt from the experience and how would it have changed your future practice?

c) Alia assumes that the new teaching accommodation with all its electronic resources has been allocated for this class because the foundation degree represents the college's highest level of provision. Would the same criteria for allocating accommodation apply in your own college? In your view, does this seem to be a fair and/or logical practice? Give clear reasons for your answer.

d) One of the learners suffers from claustrophobia. Alia clearly wasn't aware of this, despite her careful check with Learning Support. Can you think of other conditions which learners may not report as a disability and yet which could in some circumstances present barriers to their learning? What could Alia do in future to ensure that she's aware of such cases?

e) How would you evaluate the way she handled the claustrophobic learner's predicament, once the lights were back on? Is there anything you would have done differently?

f) Look at how Alia introduces herself to the class. How would you evaluate this as an introduction? Consider carefully how you usually introduce yourself to a class. Do you establish your subject specialist credentials? Would the way you introduce yourself to a class differ depending on the level or age of the learners? Explain your answer.

g) Alia finds herself facing flak from a learner about the course getting off to a slow start. This slow start is something which is not within her remit, as a subject specialist, to address. In your view, how well does she handle this situation? Would you have advised her to do anything differently? If so, what, and why?

h) Following her dialogue with Babs, she notices that most of the learners have begun to relax. Why do you think this is so?

i) She had evidently planned to open the lesson with an activity which would enable her to learn a little about the learners, including their names. Do you think she made the right decision when she chose to skip this? In your opinion, what are the advantages and disadvantages of this change of plan?

j) She then makes another change to her lesson plan, deciding to omit some group discussion. What was her reason for this? What impact did this have on the next part of the lesson?

k) Alia misjudges the learners' current level of knowledge. How could she have avoided this? What is your opinion of her response when her mistake becomes apparent? Have you ever had a similar experience, either as a subject specialist or as a learner? If so, what did you learn from it?

Activity 3

In this section we see a later part of the lesson and we have a chance to read Alia's journal entry in which she reflects on what she could have done differently. You may find it useful to compare the way she reflects on her experience with your own approach to reflection. You will see that most of her reflections have three main components: a description of the issue or incident, an analysis of how or why it arose and a reflection about how this will change her future practice.

a) What further point do you think Alia was about to add to her list?

b) She says that it is because she is an experienced teacher that she was able to identify what was going wrong. Do you think she was right? Do you think a trainee teacher or an early career teacher would equally well have been able to identify what was going wrong, and why?

c) As Alia realises, there is always a danger that a specialist in any subject or vocational area may use vocabulary that is unfamiliar to others. What are the key terms that you have to define most frequently in your own subject area? Do you always remember to do this?

Activity 4

In this short final section we see Alia and Jenni taking up Matt's case with the Assistant Principal. This is a difficult and unusual situation in which they find themselves. The following questions invite you to consider the issues about professionalism and collegiality that difficult encounters such as this can raise.

a)   Jenni knocks and enters, ignoring the sign above the door. Is she justified in doing this, in your opinion? What reasons would you give to support your answer?

b)   Gail Clifford begins by firing questions at Jenni and Alia. What do you think she is demonstrating here? Where have we seen her using this tactic before?

c)   Does Alia's defence of Matt conform to accepted standards of professional behaviour? Is there anything else she could have said in his defence? If so, what and why? She doesn't offer any criticism of Mo. Why do you think that is?

d)   Now consider what Jenni has to say in this section about Mo's accusation. Does her defence of Matt keep within the parameters of professionalism? Give reasons for your answer.

e)   How professionally does the Assistant Principal, Gail Clifford, behave throughout this exchange? What evidence can you present to support your answer?

And finally...

»   *You will find some helpful texts relating to the topics covered in this story listed under Further Reading at the back of this book.*

»   *To find out what becomes of Matt, and how Jenni copes with her teaching observation, you'll need to read on...*

Story 8 Making the most of mentoring

Chapter aims

This story will help you to reflect on:

- what you need from your mentor at various stages, from trainee teacher to experienced professional;

- how to use the mentoring relationship positively and productively;

- the range of ways in which a mentor can provide you with support;

- key factors which make for a productive mentoring relationship;

- what to do if the relationship with your mentor is not working.

Part one: Jenni and Matt talk with their mentors

Section A

Jenni watched Eleni turn off her mobile and put it away in her bag. There was a strictly enforced rule about phones in here. She had asked Eleni, her mentor, if they could meet in one of the small study rooms attached to the college library. She wanted some privacy to talk about her current predicament, and she wanted to do it somewhere where Eleni could not be distracted by emails and texts.

'Thanks', said Jenni. 'I really appreciate you giving up this time for me at such short notice.' Easily distracted Eleni might be, but she had already proved to be a supportive mentor when things got tough.

'So what's it all about?' she asked now.

'There's a complicated back story to this', said Jenni. 'But the bottom line is that Mo from Health and Social Care is going to do my peer observation and grade my teaching. And I don't want him to do it. I want you to do it. You're my mentor.'

'Well, it doesn't hurt to have feedback from someone else', said Eleni. 'He might pick up on something useful that I would miss.'

'No. No, you don't understand. He's – well, I feel a bit unprofessional saying this – but he's not a teacher whose opinion or advice I would value. And also I think he may feel some animosity towards me because he's trying to get our trainee teacher, Matt, chucked out and I've more or less told Gail Clifford that Mo's not telling the truth, and –'

'Whoa!' Eleni held up her hand. 'But she might tell him you said that.'

'Oh yes', said Jenni. 'She will. She said she was going to tell him. And then she said that he'll be grading my teaching. She's dropping me right in it. She'd have to be daft not to see that.'

'I heard', said Eleni, leaning forward and dropping her voice to a whisper, 'that they've got a thing going.'

'What thing? Who?'

'Gail Clifford, and Mo from Health and Social Care.'

Jenni stared at her. 'You're kidding!'

Eleni raised her eyebrows. 'That's what I've heard.'

'So what am I going to do?'

'I think the only thing you can do', said Eleni, 'is to have me in there, too – as your mentor. That way, if you feel his assessment of your teaching is unfair, you'll have a witness who can give a second opinion.'

'So I'd have two of you sitting there observing me?'

'I can't think of any other way around it', said Eleni.

'I was thinking that maybe I should go and have a word with the Head of School', said Jenni. 'I mean, he's my direct line manager. I could ask *him* to observe me. He'll have to do my annual review anyway. And I could ask him to tell Mo he needn't bother.'

Eleni shook her head. 'I think it's better my way.'

Jenni could feel herself wanting to cry. She couldn't let herself do that. It would look so unprofessional to burst into tears. Instead she smiled brightly and said, 'Okay. So tell me, what exactly did you hear about Mo and Gail Clifford?'

'Shhh!' Eleni glanced around, even though the room was far too small to fit anyone else in it, and leaned forward again. 'Well, I was out with Nic. You know, Nic? Have I told you about Nic?'

Many times, thought Jenni. She kept smiling and tried to look interested.

Meanwhile, Matt was also talking to his mentor. He and Alia were sitting in the refectory. It was past five o'clock and the shutters were coming down over the serving hatches. They would soon be the only two left in there.

'Would you like to talk me through again what actually happened between you and Mo?' said Alia.

Matt pushed away his mug with its dregs of cold tea and told her as much as he could remember. He'd told Alia about his encounters with Mo at the time, and he'd gone over them several times in his head since, trying to see where he'd gone wrong, how he'd rubbed the bloke up the wrong way.

'Okay', said Alia when he'd finished. 'Let me see if I've got this right.' She ticked off the points on her fingers. 'You told him you noticed some learners couldn't keep up. You pointed out the need for differentiation. You asked him for a copy of his lesson plan. So far, how does that sound to you?'

'It sounds', said Matt miserably, 'as though I'm a tutor and I'm talking to him like he's a trainee teacher.'

'Okay. And then he says he wouldn't show you his lesson plan even if he had one, in case you might pinch it. And you say –?'

'That I wouldn't want to use his poxy lesson plan anyway. Although not in those words, obviously.'

'So, do you think there might be a connection between these things and him deciding to make trouble for you?' asked Alia mildly.

Matt nodded. 'Spot on', he said. 'I've been a right plonker. Too clever for my own good.'

'You told me at the time that you thought he was trying to push your buttons. Do you think he succeeded?'

'That second time I observed him, yeah. He did.' Matt put his head in his hands.

'But, you know, everything you asked him was completely reasonable. Most colleagues here would never have responded as defensively and so negatively. Unless you told them *their* lesson was rubbish, of course.' She was trying to make him smile.

'So what shall I do?' asked Matt.

'Well, think it through. What are your options?'

Matt said nothing for a while. And then, 'The only sensible way out of this is for me to apologise to him.' He looked up at Alia. 'Don't you think so?'

'It has to be a decision you're comfortable with', she said.

'Right. Well, I'm going to offer him an apology. I'll say it's been brought to my attention that I caused him offence, and that I very much regret it, and that I'm enjoying my teacher training so much I may have come over as a bit too keen. What do you reckon?'

'It would work for me', said Alia. 'But when you make this apology it might be useful to remember that he's successfully pushed your buttons once and may well try it again. What would you do, for example, if he's not satisfied with a simple apology and decides to make you grovel?'

'Well, then', said Matt, 'I'll grovel. There's a lot at stake here. I can't throw this placement away for the sake of my pride.'

'Do you want to role play it first?' asked Alia. 'Pretend I'm Mo and practise your apology on me?'

Matt, relieved now that he'd come to a decision, smiled broadly. 'You're a brave woman!' he said.

Section B

The next day, late in the morning, Jenni was talking to Eleni again. She'd been awake most of the night, worrying. The more she thought about it, the more convinced she became that the best solution was to go and talk to the Head of School. Padraig was a supportive, approachable sort of person. She felt sure he would see the difficulty of her position and sort things out for her. The trouble was, now that her mentor had more or less said 'Don't do that', Jenni was worried that asking Padraig for help would look as though she didn't value her advice. She had no free time that day, and neither did Eleni, so they were having a rushed conversation now, hurrying together from the Pillarbox building over to their next classes in the New Block. Eleni's stride was long and Jenni found she was having to trot along to keep up.

'It's just I've been thinking', she said. 'I really don't want Mo observing me. Even with you sitting in there as well. And it's very kind of you to offer to do that. But I just think if I go to Padraig and explain and ask him to –'

'You know what'll happen if you do that, don't you?' said Eleni.

'What?'

'You'll end up being observed twice; first by Mo and me and second by Padraig. That'll be two lessons to worry about. All the planning and stuff.'

'But I'm going to ask him to do it *instead* of Mo', said Jenni. She was out of breath, what with anxiety and trying to keep up.

'And I'm telling you, he'll not do it', said Eleni, quite sharply. 'He won't go against Gail Clifford. No-one in their right mind would want to do that.'

'But that's terrible', said Jenni. 'She shouldn't be able to wage her own vendettas like this. She must be accountable to someone, surely.'

'She's accountable to the Principal', said Eleni, and added sarcastically, 'Perhaps you'd like to ask *him* to carry out your observation?'

'Perhaps I will', said Jenni grimly. She didn't like injustice, and she certainly wasn't going to let anyone walk all over her, not even scary Gail Clifford.

'I'm going up to the third floor', said Eleni, pressing the button for the lift. 'And you need to think carefully, Jenni. I mean, what's the point of having me for a mentor if you're not going to take my advice?'

Jenni took the stairs. She was wishing now that she'd handled this whole thing differently – gone to Padraig, the Head of School, straight away instead of running it past her mentor. What she really needed was to talk all this through with someone who would listen, someone who would understand the predicament she was in. Still puffing her way up the stairs, she took out her phone and texted Matt:

Pub after work?

She hesitated for only a moment and then thumbed 'send'.

Matt was talking to Alia in her office when his phone whistled at him. He ignored it. He was concentrating on the task in hand, which was reporting back to his mentor, as accurately as possible, on how his apology to Mo had gone down.

He'd checked the timetable online to see where Mo was teaching and when, and found he'd be finishing a class at 10.30 that morning, after which he'd have an hour of non-contact time. So Matt went up and waited outside the classroom. He got there early, which proved to be a useful move because Mo emerged at twenty-five past, briefcase under his arm, before the first learner was out of the door. When he saw Matt he looked a bit shifty but kept on walking.

'Mind if I walk with you?' Matt said.

Mo mumbled something that sounded like 'Whatever.'

'Listen, mate', said Matt. 'I need to talk to you. Can I buy you a brew?'

'No thanks.'

'I'll walk with you to your office, then', said Matt. 'We can have a word there.'

Mo wouldn't look at him. 'I'm busy', he said.

'I understand that, mate', said Matt. 'But this is important. And, one way or another, we're going to have this conversation. So if you slow down a bit we can have it here, and I won't have to take up any more of your time.'

Mo started walking faster. 'It's no good you threatening me', he said. 'I'm not changing my story.'

'Hey, slow down', said Matt. 'All I want is to apologise to you. I think, looking back, that I may have come over as a bit – well – over-keen, right? When my tutor says always have a lesson plan, I just assume that's what everybody does. Standard operating procedure. It's my background, you see. I'm just used to there being a right way and a wrong way. But I realise now that I can't just impose that way of thinking on everybody else. So that's why I'm apologising. And I hope we can shake on it.'

Mo kept walking. He still wouldn't meet Matt's eye. So Matt kept step alongside him, wondering where he could take it from here. His apology was genuine enough, but it wasn't going to do him any good if Mo refused to accept it.

So he persevered. 'I mean, come on, mate. What else can I say?'

Mo swerved into his shared office without breaking stride. He dumped his briefcase on a desk and turned to face Matt. There were other colleagues working in there, and this seemed to give him back the courage to bluster. 'Do you really want me to add harassment to my complaint about you?' he said.

Matt spread his hands. 'The last thing I want to do is harass you', he said. 'I just want to apologise for upsetting you, that's all. And to assure you that if I'd known you'd be upset by what I said, I never would have said it.'

A colleague on the far side of the room looked up and grinned. 'There's nothing much you *can* say to Mo without him getting upset. I'd forget about it if I were you.'

'I would', said Matt, 'except that he's made a complaint against me.' And then, realising that didn't sound good, he added quickly, 'So I know I must have been out of line.'

'I doubt it', said the colleague, still grinning. 'He hasn't spoken to me ever since I did a peer observation of him and suggested it might be nice if he used a lesson plan occasionally.'

'Really?' said Alia now, as Matt got to that point in the story. 'He actually said that?' She turned to her computer and brought last semester's peer observation schedule up on her screen. 'Pete Smith', she said. 'That'll be who it is. He did Mo's last peer obs. Good. That's useful to know. So what happened next?'

What had happened next was that another colleague, working with her back to them at the bank of computers, swivelled round in her chair and said, 'Just shake the man's hand, Mo. He's being big enough to apologise. You should try to be big enough to accept it.' And then, to Matt, 'Hi. I'm Parvinder. Mo's Head of School. And you are –?'

Matt introduced himself. He told her how much he'd enjoyed teaching Mo's class.

'Yes', she said, glancing briefly at Mo. 'I heard. The learners told me how useful they found it, too. In fact, I was thinking of passing on that feedback to Gail Clifford and telling her that we'd like you back to do a few more of your TP sessions with our HSC learners. Would you mind if I did that?'

Alia beamed at Matt. 'Result!' she said. 'So how do you feel now?'

'It's like I've been able to put down a massive weight and walk away', said Matt. 'I still can't believe my luck.'

'Luck?' said Alia. 'Don't you think it might be more to do with your hard work and careful planning and professionalism under pressure? You taught an excellent lesson. You reflected on your interactions with Mo and decided, even though he was largely in the wrong, that the professional thing for you to do would be to apologise to him. Parvinder's intervention is the result of you behaving as a professional. You earned it.'

'But I couldn't have handled it like this without your help', said Matt.

'Give yourself some credit', said Alia. 'All I've done is listen and ask a few questions.'

'But you know, Gail Clifford could still bin me', said Matt. 'She has the final say, doesn't she?'

'I think', said Alia, 'the odds are now stacked pretty well in your favour. She's a pragmatist at heart. She's unlikely to make a decision that could legitimately be questioned.'

As he left the building, Matt checked his phone. A message from Jenni. He'd been planning a long run after work to burn off some of the adrenalin, but he texted her back anyway: *ok c u there*.

Section C

It was early and so Matt and Jenni were just about the only ones in the pub. Matt was on orange juice because he was still planning a run for later – a night run, probably, from the way Jenni was going on. She'd hardly stopped talking since she walked in. Matt tried to take a leaf out of his mentor's book and listen constructively. He hadn't had a chance yet to tell Jenni that the problem with Mo looked as though it was sorting itself out. There just hadn't been an opening.

'She seems to think her role is to tell me what to do', Jenni was saying. 'I mean, sometimes that's useful. But she surely shouldn't be making my decisions for me. She should be helping me to make my own, shouldn't she?'

'Have you said this to her?' Matt asked. He thought it was the sort of question Alia would have put to him.

'I think she'd get irritable with me if I did. She snapped at me today and I was only suggesting asking Padraig to do my observation.'

'Would it be the end of the world if she did snap at you again?' said Matt. 'I mean, you're two adults. She's not your line manager or anything. So if you asserted yourself and told her what you wanted out of the relationship, what's the worst that could happen?'

Suddenly, Jenni smiled. 'I've never told you, have I, about her boyfriend obsession? She's into online dating. It's actually quite funny how she gets every conversation around to this man she's been seeing. But then sometimes – just sometimes – she turns out to be really helpful. Like, she gave me loads of information about adult learners. It must have taken her ages, and I was so grateful. I suppose what I'm going to have to do is recognise her strengths and just put up with her limitations.'

'I think you're dead right', said Matt. 'Nobody's mentor's going to be perfect.'

'Except yours!'

'Oh, yeah', he said. 'Except mine. That's right.' And they both laughed. 'So you know Eleni'll be helpful when you need specific information', said Matt. 'But when you need some help coming to a decision, you'll maybe have to turn to someone else.'

'Are you offering?' asked Jenni.

There was an awkward silence. Matt, lining up a couple of beer mats, didn't look at her. So to cover her embarrassment she asked, 'What do you reckon it is that makes Alia such a good mentor?'

'She listens', said Matt. 'She listens very carefully, and then she asks a question that helps me think more clearly about what I've just said. Me, I'm used to taking orders. But that's not her style. I mean, I was convinced at one point that my problem with Mo was clear cut, with me as the good guy and him as the one completely in the wrong. But then she got me to reflect in detail on my conversation with him and then I realised that I'd probably come over as quite aggressive and confrontational with him. That wasn't a comfortable thing to admit to myself, and I reckon if she'd just pointed it out to me, instead of getting me to see it for myself, I'd have got all indignant and rejected the idea. Then I wouldn't have apologised, and I'd still be in that mess.'

Jenni almost choked on her beer. 'You've *apologised*? To *him*?'

'Yep. And some of his colleagues heard me do it, including his line manager, who's going to tell Gail Space Invader that they want me to do more teaching for them.'

'But that's amazing!' said Jenni. 'Let me buy you another drink and we'll celebrate!'

But Matt shook his head. He explained his plans for a run. 'And anyway', he said, 'I'm not out of the woods yet. Mo could still get his way.' Jenni's smile faded and she looked miserable again, which made him feel bad. 'Come on. Cheer up', he said. 'Why don't you pretend I'm your mentor and tell me what you want out of the relationship. That'll help you to get it clear in your head before you have a word with her.'

'Hang on. I haven't agreed I'll have a word with her yet', said Jenni. 'But okay. Let me think. What would I say?' She thought for a moment. 'Right. I'd say I don't want to have to conduct important conversations with her while I'm trotting down the corridor trying to keep up with her. I want us to have space and time to talk confidentially. I want our meetings to focus on my needs, not on her concerns about her boyfriend or on college gossip. I want her to listen to me, not bulldoze me into decisions I'm not comfortable with. What else? Oh yes. I want her to give me some space in our meetings to think things through – not expect me to give instant responses. And I'd also tell her that I'm grateful for the information and tips she's given to me, but that I don't find it helpful when she orders me about. In fact, bossing me about isn't my idea of what mentoring should be at all.'

'Good one', said Matt. 'You need to have that conversation with her, Jenni.' He got up to go.

'Matt, wait a minute.' She caught hold of his sleeve. 'There's something you should know. It's something Eleni told me this morning. I don't want to burst your bubble, but she reckons that Mo and Gail Clifford are having a thing on the quiet.'

'A thing?'

'An affair.'

Matt closed his eyes and sat down again. However many km he ran now, he knew he wasn't going to sleep tonight.

Part two: Critical thinking activities

The tasks in this part of the chapter encourage you to think about what you need from your relationship with your mentor. If you currently have a formally appointed mentor you will be able to draw on your own experience and compare it to Jenni's and to Matt's. If you don't officially have a mentor, think of a colleague who has stepped informally into that role at some point in order to give you professional help or support, and use that experience as a starting point for your reflection in the activities that follow.

Activity 1

In this section we see two mentoring sessions. The following questions encourage you to evaluate and compare them in terms of effectiveness and good practice. You may find it useful to remind yourself of Matt's conversations with Mo by re-reading the relevant section of Chapter 3. This will help you to evaluate how accurately or honestly Matt is recalling them.

a)   The first half of this section describes Jenni's meeting with her mentor. How effective is Eleni being as a mentor on this occasion? It may be helpful to read this account through again in order to identify (i) the ways in which she gives positive support and (ii) the instances when she slips out of her mentoring role.

b) You will have noticed that she is very directive. She tells Jenni what to do and dismisses Jenni's idea of approaching the Head of School. Do you think Jenni finds this helpful? How might Eleni have approached this differently?

c) Jenni asks to meet somewhere where there will be *privacy to talk.* Thinking back on your own experience of being mentored, where and how were your discussions with your mentor conducted? What impact do you think this had on the quality of the mentoring relationship?

d) When talking of Jenni's teaching observation, Eleni suggests that 'feedback from someone else' might be useful. Do you agree? Have you had experience of feedback from a range of observers? If so, did you find this helpful, and in what ways?

e) Jenni says she feels 'a bit unprofessional' saying that she wouldn't much value Mo's assessment of her teaching. Do you think she *is* being unprofessional here? Give reasons for your answer.

f) In the second half of this section we find Alia mentoring Matt. Look through the account of this again and note how many of Alia's contributions to the dialogue are in the form of questions. What do you think she aims to achieve by this? In your view, does she succeed in her aim?

g) Now compare the accounts of the two mentoring sessions in their entirety, and consider the following questions: (i) Which mentor do you think was the most *directive*, giving instructions about what to do? (ii) Which mentor do you think was the most helpful to the person being mentored (the 'mentee'), and why?

h) Which of these accounts comes closest to your own experience of being mentored?

Activity 2

In section B we see Jenni and Matt talking again with their mentors. While you are answering the questions below you may find it useful to compare their experiences of mentoring with your own and to consider what makes for a positive mentoring relationship.

a) The mentoring conversation between Jenni and Eleni is taking place as they hurry to their next classes. How does this compare with your own experience of being mentored? What are the disadvantages of this sort of *on the move* mentoring? Might there be advantages too, and, if so, what are they?

b) Jenni is determined that she 'wasn't going to let anyone walk all over her.' What is your view of her attitude here? What would you do if you found yourself in her position?

c) Eleni says, 'What's the point of having me for a mentor if you're not going to take my advice?' Judging by what you have seen of her so far, what do you think Eleni understands the role of a mentor to be? Do you agree with her?

d) How might Jenni have changed the nature and outcome of this dialogue with her mentor? Think about how you might have conducted this conversation if you were in her position.

e) Consider the dialogue that takes place in this section between Matt and Mo. How would you rate each of them in terms of professionalism, and why? Do you think there was an alternative way for Matt to approach this situation? If so, what would you have advised him to try?

f) Mo threatens to add *harassment* to his complaint against Matt. Do you think he has grounds here to do this? You may find it useful to access your own institution's policy on harassment. It will provide definitions and criteria against which you can assess Matt's conduct in this situation.

g) When Matt thanks Alia for her help, she says, 'All I've done is listen and ask a few questions.' In your view, is this an accurate summary of her approach to mentoring? If you think that her mentoring of Matt is a more complex process than her modest summary of it suggests, how *would* you describe it?

h) Again, compare the accounts of the two mentoring sessions in their entirety, and consider which mentor, in your view, was the more helpful, and why.

i) Which of the two accounts in this section comes closest to your own experience of being mentored?

Activity 3

In the third section we see Jenni and Matt discussing their experiences of being mentored and reflecting on what *good* mentoring should look like. They also raise the question of how much responsibility the *mentee* should take for making the mentoring relationship work.

a) Matt tries to help Jenni by doing something he has noticed that his mentor does, which is to 'listen constructively'. What do you think he means by this? Do you agree with him that it is helpful to have a mentor who can do this? Is this a skill you have recognised in your own mentor? Do you yourself *listen constructively* when colleagues are talking to you about their teaching experiences?

b) Jenni complains that her mentor, 'shouldn't be making my decisions for me. She should be helping me to make my own.' Do you agree with her? Why might it be important for you as a trainee teacher or a newly appointed teacher to be supported in making your own decisions?

c) Matt asks Jenni whether she has considered asserting herself and telling her mentor what she needs from the mentoring relationship. To what extent have you been able to shape your relationship with your own mentor or mentors? Do you think it is important, as a mentee, to be allowed to do this, and, if so, why?

d) Matt describes the skills and qualities which, in his view, make Alia a good mentor. Do you agree that these are important to good mentoring? Have you noticed from your reading of this chapter and earlier ones anything else which in your view makes Alia an effective mentor?

e) What do you think Matt himself brings to the mentoring relationship which contributes to its success?

f) Jenni lists a number of issues which she would ideally like to raise with her mentor. How would you order them in terms of priority? Do any of these issues apply to your own experience of being mentored? If so, how and what might you be able to do about it?

g) In your view, was Jenni acting within the boundaries of acceptable professional behaviour when she repeated to Matt what her mentor had told her about Mo and Gail Clifford? What reasons would you give to support your answer?

And finally...

» *You will find some helpful texts relating to mentoring and being mentored listed under Further Reading at the back of this book.*

» *Will Matt win his case? Will Jenni find the courage to speak to Eleni about how their mentoring relationship is failing her? To find out what happens you'll need to read on...*

Story 9　Good professional: good colleague

Chapter aims

This story will help you to reflect on:

- the skills needed to negotiate the often complex relationships with colleagues, mentors and line managers;

- the importance of establishing and maintaining mutual respect in interactions with colleagues, mentors and learners;

- the importance of professionalism and respect in all teacher–learner interactions;

- the importance of teachers behaving as models of appropriate behaviour;

- the importance of maintaining a professional manner in difficult or confrontational situations – whether these are with learners or with colleagues.

Part one: Professionalism and respect

Section A

As Matt was leaving his flat the next morning, his phone rang. He considered letting it go to message. This was his teacher training day – his day for being a student – and he had to be at the morning session by 0900 hours prompt. It had been impressed on them all by their teacher trainer that punctuality was a key aspect of professionalism, and that although they may also be learners for this particular day of the week, they were nevertheless still teachers in training and were expected to conduct themselves accordingly. Matt respected rules. He had no intention of being late. So he answered the phone as he strode down the path, and found himself talking to Gail Clifford's PA.

'Ms Clifford would like to see you in her office at 9.30', she said.

'What? This morning? Why? What's it about?'

'I'm sorry', said the PA's voice smoothly. 'I don't have that information.'

Matt turned the corner and speeded up as he approached the bus stop. 'I can't come in this morning', he said. 'It's my training day. I've got to be at –'

'Ms Clifford wanted you to know that it's both important and urgent that she sees you this morning', said the PA.

Matt's heart sank. This was it, then. He was getting binned. If that was the case, there was no point him turning up for his training day. If he didn't have any teaching he couldn't remain on the course. Well, he thought, at least she was going to have to look him in the eye to do it. 'Okay', he said into his phone. 'Tell her I'll be there.'

He must have looked a bit grim because he noticed the woman next to him in the queue edging a couple of steps away from him. He tried flashing her a smile but that seemed to alarm her even more. So he just stared miserably at his shoes and waited for the bus to arrive.

Alia was with the foundation degree group again that morning. The session was going well. She'd got off to a much better start this time. For a start, she'd not plunged the room into darkness or induced any panic attacks. In fact, this small group of adult learners seemed to have warmed to her – with the exception of one male learner with a heavily bandaged hand, who seemed to be glowering at her every time she looked in his direction. She had discovered that his name was Colin, and she made a point of using it frequently, smiling at him and trying to draw him in. But he sat unsmiling with his arms folded awkwardly, bandage on display, and his chin up. Alia, who was pretty good at reading body language, got the message loud and clear: he had a problem with her and he wanted her to know it.

She knew from long experience that the only way to deal with this sort of thing was to persevere in being pleasant towards him; to treat him with the same respect she was showing for every other learner and generally to model the sort of behaviour she expected from him. It never paid, she knew, to engage in acrimonious exchanges with learners, or to respond to a learner's obvious dislike by showing that you didn't like them either. She'd seen that sort of mistake made from time to time when she'd been doing lesson observations. That approach never resolved anything. She usually advised colleagues very strongly not to take that sort of learner behaviour personally. 'Nine times out of ten it's not about you', she would say. 'It's about them and something they're carrying over from negative experiences of teachers in the past.' So now she was determined to take her own advice. Fixing Colin with a sunny smile, she asked him whether he had any questions so far.

'Yes', he said. 'As a matter of fact, I have. Don't they give you lot any IT training before they send you into a classroom?'

Oh, so that was it, thought Alia. He was still obsessing about that disastrous start to her first session with them. She kept her smile in place. 'Yes, they do, Colin. But I'm afraid the first time I met you was my first time in this room. And, unfortunately, none of the switches on this console are labelled.' She'd explained this all before, of course, but was not going to point this out to him. 'Come and have a look', she said, beckoning him. 'I think you'll see what I mean.'

If she could get him out of his seat she might be able to snap him out of that defensive pose he was adopting. Inviting him into what was seen as *the teacher's space* was a way of saying, *Look, we're both on the same side here*. But Colin wasn't having any of it. He simply continued to glare at her.

'No? Okay then', she said. 'Any questions about what we've covered so far in this lesson? No? Anyone else?'

She fielded useful questions from a couple of the other learners. She could sense the general embarrassment over Colin's behaviour, but so long as the other learners saw that it was causing her no obvious difficulty – as long as she remained upbeat and apparently relaxed about the situation – the problem would be contained. And so she made sure that she maintained the same degree of eye contact with Colin as with the rest of the group, knowing that there was always a great temptation for a teacher to avoid looking at a learner whom they feared would cause trouble. If she avoided meeting his eye Colin would recognise, consciously or not, that he had unsettled her. And, if that happened, the battle he was trying to have with her would escalate.

It was a two-hour session, and she decided to give them a break midway through. As adults with multiple responsibilities they clearly appreciated the chance to grab a coffee, most of them having rushed to get to college on time as well as deliver kids to school or look in on elderly parents. Alia's primary reason for calling a break, however, was so that she could have a quiet word with Colin and see if she could put things right. But Colin was out of the door and on his way down to the cafeteria before she could catch him, and if she called after him it would defeat the object of speaking to him privately.

Tim, the learner who had suffered an attack of claustrophobia when the lights went out during her first lesson with them, stayed behind. Alia was studying her lesson plan, considering how she would adjust it to accommodate the break, when Tim came up to her hesitantly and asked if he could have a word. 'It's about Colin', he said.

Alia's heart sank. 'Oh?', she said, hoping she sounded unconcerned. 'What about him?'

Tim looked very uncomfortable. 'He keeps telling me I ought to threaten to sue you', he said.

'*Sue* me?'

'For setting off my claustrophobia. But –' he added hastily, 'I'd never do that, obviously. It wasn't your fault and I was fine, and – well – I'm not like that.'

Alia wasn't sure what to say. So she nodded and smiled. 'Thank you', she said. 'But, Tim, if he's making you feel uncomfortable you should go and have a word with Student Support Services and –'

'Well, actually, the thing that's bothering me is I think he's trying to encourage me to *blackmail* you.'

Alia just stared at him.

'I mean', he said, 'he says I should threaten to sue you and offer to settle if you give me some money.'

'Good grief. Well, I appreciate you telling me this, Tim. Frankly, I'm shocked. Are you sure he said that?'

Tim looked hurt. 'Yes', he said. 'Honestly. And he said he'd done it already with someone else here – got money off them, I mean.'

Alia took a deep breath. 'Okay, Tim' she said. 'Well we don't know whether he's telling the truth about that, and I can't do anything right now because people'll be coming back any minute. But don't worry. I'll have a word with him at the end of the lesson.'

Jenni, meanwhile, was sitting with her Head of School, Padraig, in the small seminar room near the open office.

'Yeah, that's fine', he was saying. 'I'm happy to observe you. But I'll have to check first whether someone else is down to do it.'

'They are', said Jenni. 'That's the trouble. That's why I've come to see you. Mo's down to do it. But I'd rather it was you.'

There was a pause. Then, 'Any particular reason?' asked Padraig.

What should she say? She knew it was important to be professional about this. 'I'd really value your view on my teaching', she said. 'Especially as you're my line manager. And it'll be useful for when you do my annual review, won't it?'

Padraig nodded. 'That makes sense. And is it okay with your mentor if I do it?'

Jenni framed her reply carefully. 'She's offered to do it', she said. 'But she'd probably be grateful if you did it. She's very busy. And', she added, trying to be as honest as possible, 'she could always do it with you – a paired observation. That'd be good for me, too.'

'Excellent', said Padraig. 'Leave it with me, then, Jenni. And I'll look forward to observing you. You can find all the forms and stuff on the intranet.'

Section B

When the green light came on, Matt squared his shoulders and walked smartly into Gail Clifford's office. He'd decided to take it on the chin. If she was going to bin him he wasn't going to plead this time. He would just have to deal with it and try to find some other way into the profession.

And so her greeting took him by surprise. 'Matt!' she beamed. 'Thank you for coming in at such short notice. I've a favour to ask you. Would you like a seat?'

Confused, he sat down in the visitor's chair. A favour? What was going on now?

'We've got two staff away sick', she said. 'You've met them. You've taught classes for them. Paul over in Motor Vehicle, and Mo. You were rather popular with both lots of learners, I understand. So I'd like you do some cover for us while Paul and Mo are away. You'll be paid, of course.'

Because this wasn't at all what he'd been expecting, it took Matt a few seconds to take it in. He realised he was staring at her with his mouth open. He closed it, cleared his throat and managed to come up with a sensible question, 'Starting when?' he said.

'Now. This morning. There's a ten o'clock class of Paul's – you've met them already, I think. And Mo's twelve o'clock group. I don't think you've seen them before. The Head of School would like you to do your first aid session with them – the one you did with the other class.'

'Normally I'd say yes straight away', said Matt. 'But today's my teacher training day and –'

'Oh, it won't hurt to miss one', said Gail Clifford, dismissing the idea with a wave of her hand. 'They wouldn't expect you to turn down an opportunity to do some real teaching.'

Was that really true, Matt wondered?

He found the Assistant Principal far less intimidating when seated. She couldn't invade any-one's space while she was in her chair – unless it had casters. He sneaked a look. Nope. He was safe.

'I really would be very grateful', she said now. 'I've a lot on my plate at the moment, and if I could just get this cover sorted out… I've got a burial to arrange, you see.' And to Matt's hor-ror he saw her eyes fill with tears.

'Oh', he said. 'Right. I'm sorry to hear that. Of course I'll do the cover. Is it…was it…?'

'I didn't expect to lose him so soon', she said, and her tears spilled over. 'He couldn't walk far these last few weeks', she said.

Matt nodded sympathetically. He'd never thought of her with a husband. It made her more human, somehow.

'And of course', she said, 'that meant he got constipated.'

Although this was certainly more than Matt wanted to know, he maintained his sympathetic expression, and started thinking quickly about how he could get out of the room.

'In some ways I suppose it's a good thing', she continued, drying her eyes. 'He had a very nasty temper. It was age, I suppose.'

Matt nodded slowly. An older man. Who'd have thought? 'Well', he said, shifting in his chair, 'I'd better –'

'I wasn't able to leave him on his own these last two weeks', she said. 'So I've been bringing him into work with me. I've been letting him lie down under my desk.'

Matt stared at her. 'Under your desk? Really? Right. Well, I'd better be off now and –'

'And that was all fine', she continued. 'He was no trouble at all. If I had to go to a meeting I just gave him a biscuit and that kept him happy.'

Matt stood, nodded, smiled and began backing towards the door.

'And then last week I'm afraid he got fed up with being under the desk and struggled out and bit a student. Rather badly. I'm afraid I had to hit him quite hard to make him let go.'

Matt was groping for the door handle. Granted, she was an odd woman. But it sounded as though her husband had been even odder.

'Yes', she said sadly. 'I suspect, if he hadn't died, I would have been obliged to arrange euthanasia.'

'Is that legal?' said Matt, feeling now that he'd personally got away quite lightly.

She frowned at him. 'Of course', she said. 'But I'd have found it very hard. He was such good company – until he turned nasty, that is.'

'I have to go now', said Matt, backing out, 'if I'm going to take that 10 o'clock class.'

'Thank you so much', said Gail Clifford. 'And thank you for listening to me ramble on. You've been very supportive.'

Of course he had, thought Matt, as he jogged across to the Motor Vehicle building. As if he'd dare not be.

At the end of the lesson Alia went over and engaged Colin in conversation before he could escape. She asked him some general questions about how he was enjoying the course and what work he had been doing previously, until the rest of the class had left the room. He'd been stuffing his file in his bag and struggling with his coat while answering her in monosyllables and avoiding any eye contact. She made a move to help him with the coat, hampered as he was by his bandaged hand, but he shrugged irritably away from her.

'Colin', she said, 'Tim tells me you're still upset about me accidentally turning the lights out.'

'*I'm* not upset', he said crossly. 'It's him who should be upset. You could have given him a heart attack. It was gross incompetence.'

'But he's not upset', said Alia. 'He understands that it was just one of those things. But it's clear that *you're* upset. You're still very angry about it. I can see you are.'

'He should bloody sue you.'

'Yes, Tim told me you'd said that. And he told me that you're making him uncomfortable by that sort of talk. He's fine with what happened. But you're clearly not. And so I'm wondering whether it would make you feel better if you made a complaint about it. And then the incident can be investigated and we can all put it behind us.'

'You think you can patronise me?' said Colin. 'If it's investigated, Tim'll just tell them he's fine and that it wasn't important.'

'Well, I suppose that's what I'm getting at, really', said Alia. 'He doesn't think it's important, so why do you?' She was keeping her voice calm and steady, but could see that Colin was getting angrier. His face was red.

'Do you have any idea what it costs to do this course?' he demanded.

'Of course I do', said Alia.

Colin leaned towards her, his mouth twisted in a sneer. 'It's alright for you, on your fat salary. Well, I wouldn't still be here – I wouldn't be able to afford the fees –if your Assistant Principal's dog hadn't taken a bite out of my arm. What do you think of that, eh?'

Alia frowned. 'You've completely lost me, I'm afraid', she said.

'Well, she's not supposed to have it on the premises, is she? And when it bloody bites somebody on top of that, well, she's going to want to keep it quiet, isn't she?'

'So let me get this straight', said Alia. 'You're finding it hard to pay the course fees and you want me to give you money to keep the incident with the lights quiet? But that makes no sense, Colin. I've just suggested that if it would make you feel better you should report it.'

'You think you're so clever', snarled Colin.

'All I'm saying to you, Colin, is please stop making Tim feel uncomfortable. Otherwise it'll be me who takes this further. Do we understand one another?'

Colin scooped up his bag with his good arm and stormed out of the room.

Jenni put her head around the door of Eleni's office, half hoping she wouldn't be there. But there she was, over at the shared computer, chatting with a couple of colleagues. It was an open office, so there was nowhere private to talk. Jenni hoped this would work in her favour. If Eleni was fed up with her for arranging an observation with Padraig she would at least have to remain civil and polite about it.

When they were sitting at Eleni's desk, Jenni plunged straight in. 'I've been to see Padraig', she said, 'and he's going to do my obs instead of Mo.'

'I see.' Eleni's phone chirruped at her. She took it out and prodded at it with a manicured finger.

Jenni shifted awkwardly in her chair. Should she carry on her explanation, or wait until Eleni had finished checking her message? She waited for what seemed like a very long time before saying, 'You could sit in as well. A joint one. That would be good.'

'I don't believe it', said Eleni.

Jenni's heart sank. 'I'm really sorry', she said. 'I know you didn't want me to ask him, but I just couldn't see the point of having Mo observe me.'

'What?' said Eleni. 'What are you talking about? Just a minute.' She prodded her phone a second time and then looked up again. 'Mo can't do your obs anyway', she said. 'He's off sick.'

'Oh.' Jenni felt an enormous relief. 'Is that what the text's about?'

'The text? No. That's from Nic. Honestly, I just can't believe how weird he's being.'

'So will you be able to observe me jointly with Padraig?' Jenni asked. 'It's tomorrow, eleven o'clock.'

'Uh huh, uh huh', said Eleni absently. She was poking at her phone again.

'See you then', said Jenni, and left. All that anxiety about having the conversation! She needn't have worried at all. Things had worked out after all. She felt a twinge of guilt about being relieved that Mo was sick. But the greatest relief, in a way, was the realisation that she was clearly very low on Eleni's list of priorities. Hopefully this meant that Eleni wouldn't mind very much when Jenni requested a different mentor, which was what she now planned to do.

Section C

When Matt got into the workshop, he recognised one or two of the lads from his previous visit. He was shocked all over again by how young they looked, and he had to remind himself that these were still school kids, getting some experience of vocational education as part of their Key Stage 4 curriculum. Something that struck him now – that he hadn't really picked up on the first time because it was all so new to him – was the fact that there were no girls in the group at all. It was unusual, surely, in this day and age, for vocational choice or interest to be so heavily gendered, and he wondered whether this gender bias originated with the school or the college.

It was obvious that some of the lads recognised him, too. The general ruckus and mayhem had died down a bit as he walked in, and a number of them were now watching him warily. A quick headcount told him that they were all present – punctuality being one of the benefits of having them bussed in from school, he supposed. There'd been no time to write a lesson plan, of course, and very little time even to work out a plan in his head as he walked across from Gail Clifford's office to here, his mind occupied with the weirdness of that last conversation. There was no scheme of work, nothing to tell him what had been covered already and what was yet to be done. Having met the teacher, Paul, a few weeks earlier, he'd known not to expect any useful documentation. So he'd have to find out from the lads themselves what they'd been doing, and make this a revision and assessment session.

He speeded up his pace as he headed across the workshop floor towards them. The learners fell silent, watching his approach nervously.

'Good morning, gentlemen', he said briskly.

A few of them muttered 'good morning' back.

'Let's try that again, shall we? Good morning, gentlemen.'

This time the response was an almost unanimous 'good morning', tailing off into 'Mr Er…' from some of them, and even, from one or two, 'sir'.

'We're not at school now', said Matt. 'We're at work. This is a workshop. You're here to learn about the world of work. So, let's say you're working here and I'm the boss. What would you call me?'

One of the lads said something under his breath and one or two others around him sniggered. Another said, 'Boss. We'd call you boss, innit.' And he looked around, grinning.

'Good one', said Matt. 'That'll do me. So let's try one more time. Good morning, gentlemen.'

'Good morning, Boss', chanted the learners, all of them grinning now.

'Okay. I want you in groups of three and I'm going to give you three minutes to decide the most useful thing you've learnt so far on this course. Time starts –' he checked his watch, '– NOW.' Then, dropping his voice, he said to the lad who'd muttered earlier, 'But not you. You can tell me now. What's the most useful thing you've learnt? The rest of you, get on with it. Time's ticking.'

'Nothing', said the learner, sullenly.

'Name?'

'Will.'

'Will what?'

'Will, Boss.'

Matt smiled. 'No, I mean what's your last name?'

'Dent.'

'Okay, Mr Dent. You say you've not learnt anything useful yet, right. Well, you're going to learn something now, because I'm going to tell you something very important, and it's this, Are you ready? It's never, ever snigger when your boss asks you a question. Because making your mates laugh isn't worth losing your job for. Got it?'

'Yes. I mean, yes, Boss.' Will Dent was red in the face. Matt didn't want to embarrass him further.

'Okay, Mr Dent. You can relax. Go and join those three over there.'

The learners' reports of what they'd found most useful varied from theoretical stuff about internal combustion to very practical skills such as changing a tyre. This feedback was delivered in a remarkably serious way. He'd expected some facetious comments and some joking about, but they seemed to be happy to mirror his own brisk, businesslike approach. It proved a useful activity, giving him a fairly clear idea of what they'd covered and in what depth, and what they'd got out of it. Not bad, he thought, considering he'd been forced to think on his feet. He'd picked up from watching their discussion in threes that some of them didn't seem to know each other very well. It turned out that the group was composed of Year 10 learners from three separate local schools, which explained that; so he got them into two mixed teams and gave them a revision quiz. When they came to any questions no one could answer, he used that as a teaching and learning opportunity.

Part two: Critical thinking activities

The following tasks encourage you to reflect carefully about the conduct of relationships and interactions within your working environment, with colleagues, managers, mentors and learners, and about the importance of professionalism.

You may find it useful to compare the way Matt, Alia and Jenni handle the situations they find themselves in, and to how you would behave in similar circumstances.

Activity 1

In this first section, we have a glimpse of how three of our characters start their day.

a)   Matt has been told that punctuality is a key aspect of professionalism. Why do you think this has been identified as an important issue? Do you agree that punctuality in a teacher is important? Are you always punctual to classes?

b)   We are told that Alia is skilled at reading body language. Colin sits 'unsmiling with his arms folded and his chin up.' Would you put the same interpretation on this as Alia does? What other elements of body language might indicate that a learner is feeling confrontational?

c)   Alia believes that 'the only way to deal with this sort of thing was to persevere in being pleasant towards him.' Do you agree? How would you handle this situation?

d)   Alia advises colleagues not to take negative learner behaviour personally. Think of a time when you have experienced negative behaviour from a learner. Did you take that incident personally? Would you have found Alia's advice, and her rationale for it, helpful in dealing with that situation? Give clear reasons for your answer.

e) The question Colin asks Alia can be seen as both confrontational and aggressive. How would you have responded in this situation? What is your evaluation of Alia's response (eg, inviting him to inspect the console), and why?

f) Alia says that it's a great temptation for a teacher to avoid looking at a learner whom they fear will cause trouble. Do you recognise this from your own experience?

g) Alia calls a break so that she can speak privately with Colin. What do you think she hopes to achieve? What is your evaluation of her strategy and why?

h) Despite her mentor's advice to the contrary, Jenni goes to see Padraig and asks him to observe her. In your view, is Jenni behaving professionally here? What is your evaluation of the way she conducts herself in the meeting with Padraig? What would you have done in this situation?

Activity 2

Section B gives us an account of three awkward scenarios. In the first, Matt expects the worst from his meeting with Gail Clifford. Instead, he is pleasantly surprised by the outcome, although the encounter becomes bizarre and embarrassing for him. The second is a potentially confrontational situation between Alia and Colin, and the third is a very difficult meeting between Jenni and her mentor, Eleni. Each of these provides an opportunity for you to reflect on what you consider to be appropriate and professional behaviour in difficult or potentially confrontational interactions.

a) Gail Clifford pressures Matt to cover for absent colleagues despite the fact that this will mean missing his teacher training day. In your view, is she justified in doing this? Is Matt right to accept? If you were in Matt's position, would you have agreed to do the teaching, and why? What are the advantages and the disadvantages for Matt in agreeing to cover these classes on his training day?

b) Matt doesn't realise that Gail Clifford is talking about her dog, and therefore what she's saying causes him confusion and some embarrassment. In your view, how well does he conduct himself in this situation?

c) Gail Clifford becomes emotional and *unloads* her distress by confiding in Matt. In your view, does she overstep the bounds of professional behaviour here? Does the definition of a 'supportive colleague' include the expectation that they will listen sympathetically to another's personal distress? (You may find it useful to think back to the disclosures of Jenni's mentor before deciding on your response to this question.)

d) Jenni decides to tell Eleni straight away, with no preamble, that she has acted against her advice. In your view, was this the best approach? How would you have broached this with your mentor?

e) We discover that Jenni is planning to request a different mentor. Do you think she is wise to do this? What are the reasons for your answer? If Eleni were your mentor, would you request a change and why?

f) In your view, who is responsible for the failure of this mentoring relationship? Should Jenni bear some responsibility for it, and if so, why?

Activity 3

In this section we see Matt thrown in to teach a class at the last possible minute with no opportunity to plan a lesson and no available documentation or scheme of work for guidance.

a) Given these unusual circumstances, how would you rate Matt's performance? What are his strengths in this situation?

b) If you were giving him feedback on the way he teaches and supports learning in this lesson, is there anything you would advise him to reflect upon or reconsider? If so, what would it be, and why?

c) Have you ever experienced an instance when you have been asked to teach a class with little or no notice? If so, how did you handle this? What did you learn about your own strengths and development needs? If this has never happened to you, imagine a scenario in which you have been put in this position. What would be your main concern, and why?

d) Matt addresses the learners formally, for example as 'Mr Dent', and addresses them collectively as 'gentlemen'. Why do you think he does this?

e) Matt observes that 'Mr Dent' is embarrassed. Was this Matt's intention, do you think? What is your evaluation of this teacher–learner conversation?

f) Matt notices that the group of learners is exclusively male. To what extent, if any, is a gender bias apparent in specific vocational areas in your own college? How does (i) the college marketing material and (ii) the choice of learning resources and materials address this?

And finally...

» *You will find some helpful texts relating to mentoring and being mentored listed under Further Reading at the back of this book.*

» *To find out what happens next, you'll need to read on...*

Story 10 Showing what you can do: performing well in lesson observations

Chapter aims

This story will help you to reflect on:

- the skills needed to plan and present a lesson which will demonstrate to an observer your best possible example of good practice;

- some key points to bear in mind when planning a lesson that is to be observed;

- the importance of careful planning for an observation;

- the importance of preparing all required documentation and having it ready for the observer;

- how a lesson observation can best be used as a learning experience for the teacher;

- why it is important to reflectively evaluate your own teaching as well as to consider and act positively on feedback from your observer/s;

- effective and appropriate ways of giving and receiving feedback;

- the professional etiquette, interactions and behaviours appropriate to a formal lesson observation;

- the importance of tolerance and empathy in professional interactions.

Part one: Matt and Jenni are being observed

Section A

Jenni was thanking her lucky stars that she'd remembered to pack a sandwich and an apple. Although she had an hour's non-teaching, admin period at midday, she wouldn't have the time to go down to the refectory. She had to go over her plan and resources and documentation for her observed teaching session at 1pm. She sat at her desk in the office, trying to shut out all the conversations going on around her. The class she was going to be observed teaching was part of an adult Access to Higher Education course. She had got off to a tricky start with them earlier in the term but, thanks partly to a useful list of tips from her mentor, she had now built up a good working relationship with them and she'd been looking forward to her sessions with them. When she'd originally identified them as the class she'd like to be observed teaching, it was because she was still unsure of herself as a teacher of adults and she was keen to get some feedback and advice. Now she was pleased that this was the class her Head of School would observe – for quite a different reason: because she was fairly confident that it would go well and that he'd be seeing her at her best.

She knew that a good lesson plan was essential to a successful observation. She checked hers over one more time. She was using the layout required by the college. This provided the following headings:

Time	Topic/ outcome	Teacher activity	Learner activity	Assessment	Resources	Differentiation

She personally would have liked to add a column which would allow her to identify opportunities for the learners to practise or demonstrate communication or numeracy skills, but she had mentioned this in the written rationale – a piece of documentation she was required to provide – which explained the lesson plan with reference both to the learners' characteristics and needs, and to the scheme of work of which it formed a part.

In terms of being observed, it was the *Time* column on the lesson plan that was the one that worried her the most. She knew it was essential that a teacher could accurately estimate how long each component of a lesson would take, so that they didn't try to cram too much in or end up finishing well before the lesson was supposed to end. But sometimes she had found it necessary to be a bit flexible, if a discussion really took off, for example. And then, to accommodate that, she'd simply have to adjust the time she'd planned to spend on some other part of the lesson. In her view, a certain amount of flexibility could be justified if it was in response to learner needs and enthusiasms. But would her observer, Padraig, see it that way? Normally, if she wasn't being observed, she would leave most of the *Time* column blank. But she couldn't do that today. She had to put precise timings in, and it felt a bit like giving a hostage to fortune.

The *Topic/outcome* column was straightforward. She knew which section of the scheme of work she was covering today, so it was just a case of pasting those topics and outcomes in. However, the *Teacher activity* and *Learner activity* columns were where she had an opportunity to really show what she could do. For a lesson that learners would find engaging and challenging it was important that there was plenty of learner activity. She remembered when she first started teaching practice as a trainee teacher; then it had seemed natural to assume that a lesson is all about what a teacher does. It was only with experience and the advice of her excellent teacher training tutor that she came to realise that it was the learning, not the teaching, which ultimately mattered. A teacher could put on a stunning performance, deliver a lecture like a stand-up comedian, but it didn't count for anything unless learners had actually learnt what they were supposed to by the end of it. So in her lesson plan she had kept teacher activity to a minimum. The column in question looked like this:

Teacher activity
Recap of the previous session
Introduce today's topic with Q&A to ascertain learners' current level of understanding
Brief exposition with PowerPoint slides
Briefing for group task
Facilitate role allocation
Facilitate task/observe/Q&A
Chair feedback
Chair questions/plenary

In the parallel *Learner activity* column, she wanted to make it clear that learners were expected to be actively engaged – listening, note-taking, asking and answering questions – even when she, the teacher, was giving formal input. So the learner column looked like this:

Learner activity
Listen. Ask and answer questions
Listen. Ask and answer questions. Make notes
Listen. Ask and answer questions. Make notes
Listen. Ask and answer questions. Make notes
Decide and agree roles within small groups
Carry out the small-group task
Give feedback to the group as a whole
Ask other groups questions, and answer questions about their own group's findings

She wasn't happy with the first half of it. She'd wanted to capture the fact that she expected the learners to be taking active responsibility for their learning through questioning and note-taking, even when she was standing at the front presenting information to them. But somehow, on the page, it just looked a rather boring and repetitive list of activities that completely failed to convey the spirit of her planned lesson. But she couldn't think of any way to usefully change it, and anyway she had emailed all the documentation to Padraig earlier. So she would just have to keep her fingers crossed that his observation of the actual lesson would bring all this to life for him.

With only a few minutes left, she drew out of her bag a clear A4 plastic wallet, inside which was a much-folded and rather tattered one page handout. It was a list of things to remember when teaching an observed lesson, given to her by her first teacher training tutor. She had copied this list on to her tablet long ago, but there was something enormously reassuring about actually holding this original battered piece of paper in her hand. It brought back the warm glow of confidence that her tutor had given her, and rebooted her enthusiasm for teaching that sometimes sank a bit low on bad days. The list was headed *Showing What You Can Do: A checklist for your observed teaching practice*; and it looked like this:

- Look happy to be there! If you *look* happy it will help you to relax and *feel* happy.

- Welcome and introduce your observer and seat them where they have a clear view of the room but – if possible – not in the direct eyeline of the learners. You don't want your learners to be distracted.

- Show you are enthusiastic about your subject/topic. If you are not enthusiastic, how can you expect your learners to be?

- Make sure you have clear outcomes/objectives for the lesson – *and that the learners know what these are*.

- Make sure the outcomes are achievable in the time available.

- Make sure the outcomes are appropriate to the learners' level of ability and prior knowledge/understanding.

- Choose learning methods/strategies that are appropriate to the learners' ability and to the subject you are teaching.

- Choose learning methods/strategies/activities that the learners will enjoy.

- Show the observer that you know your learners' names – use them!

- Ensure that your plan creates clear opportunities to assess the learners against the outcomes, and to give them clear and constructive feedback on their achievement.

- Don't make over-elaborate use of resources in an effort to impress. Remember, it is the quality of learning that is important.

- Where possible, don't make your lesson entirely dependent on technology. Technology can fail! So always have a back-up plan.

- Make it clear in your plan that you have taken into account the possible need for differentiation.

- Stick to your timings as closely as possible, but recognise the advantage of being flexible if the real need arises. Your observer will appreciate your ability to think on your feet.

- And finally: Be prepared. *Always* have a plan B!

Jenni slid the plastic wallet back into her bag. She gathered up hard copies of her lesson documentation, stood up, took a deep breath, and set off to be observed.

Section B

Matt stood in front of Mo's class trying very hard not to think too much about the fact that Gail Clifford was sitting there at the back of the room watching him, her pen poised above her clipboard. He hadn't met this class before, so his first concern was to learn a few names while he discovered who knew what about his topic: emergency first aid. The lesson he was going to teach was the same one his mentor had observed him teaching to a parallel class, and so – by an enormous stroke of luck – he had a copy of the lesson plan and all the other documentation with him on a data stick in his bag. This meant he'd been able to provide Gail Clifford with all the necessary paperwork despite the fact that this whole situation – the teaching and her observation of it – was a last minute arrangement. The lesson had gone down very well last time, and, he told himself, there was no reason why it shouldn't do so again, despite that steely gaze from the back of the room.

Once the learning objectives were up on the screen and the initial question and answer session was in full swing, he could feel himself beginning to relax. The learners were relaxing, too: becoming less reluctant to respond to his questioning, beginning to smile, uncrossing their arms and looking as though they might begin to enjoy themselves.

'Okay', Matt said. 'Before we go any further, have *you* got any questions for *me*?'

One of the lads by the window called out, 'What's in the box?'

'You'll see in a minute', said Matt. 'And I'm going to ask you to raise a hand, please, if you've got a question, so I can make sure no one misses out.'

A young woman seated near the front raised her hand.

'Yes, Britney?'

'Are you going to be our teacher now?'

'Just for this lesson, Britney.'

There was a collective *Ohhhh* of disappointment from the class.

Another girl at Britney's table raised her hand. Matt nodded at her to go ahead. What she wanted to tell him, she said, was that they didn't like Mo and they wanted to know who they had to ask in order to have Matt instead on a permanent basis. There were murmurs of agreement. All eyes were on him to see how he would respond to this, and not least Gail Clifford's. He could almost feel them boring into him.

He really could have done without the learners bringing up this sort of thing. But, on the other hand, he thought to himself, at least it was an opportunity to demonstrate to the Assistant Principal that he would handle this in a professional manner.

'Okay, that'll do', he said. 'These are inappropriate questions. They have no bearing on the topic we're working on, and what you're doing here is taking up time that we could be using in much more interesting ways. I want you all to have an opportunity to get acquainted with what's in this box –' he nodded towards the case containing the resuscitation dummy –'and if we're going to do that, we need to crack on. So let me just make this clear: I've got extensive professional experience of emergency first aid, but as far as being a teacher's concerned, I'm still in training. So you need to wait until I've got my qualification, and *then* you can ask the college to give me a permanent job.'

The learners laughed. He noticed that Gail Clifford, too, was smiling. And that, he thought to himself, wasn't something you saw very often.

From that point the lesson proceeded smoothly. As far as he could judge, it went as well – if not even better – than the first time he'd taught it, to the parallel group. Every learner had an opportunity to demonstrate whether they could do what the learning outcomes required, and in the final question and answer session with which he closed the lesson the learners stuck strictly to the subject. At the very end, several came up and thanked him. So he was feeling pretty upbeat when Gail Clifford rose from the back of the room and walked over, coming to a halt just a little too close, as usual. But, without a smile and without a comment on his lesson, positive or otherwise, she simply said, 'I have to leave now. Come to me at the end of the afternoon and I'll give you some feedback.'

Section C

Jenni's observed lesson, meanwhile, was just about to begin. The trouble was, Padraig hadn't shown up yet, and so she was struggling with the dilemma of whether to start on time – which was something she felt was very important in sending the right message to learners; or whether to wait a few minutes and hope that Padraig arrived as soon as possible. If she started now, he would miss seeing her introduction and her recap of the previous lesson, both of which she felt were crucial to the overall success of her lesson plan. If she waited, she would be wasting the time of these adult learners whose busy lives and multiple commitments made every moment precious. Thinking quickly on her feet, she decided to spend a few minutes discussing with the class one of the day's headlines she'd spotted on the front of Bob's customary newspaper. The headline related usefully to a topic they'd been discussing the previous week. She was relieved, therefore, when Padraig came through door, breathless and apologetic, that it was to find the class engaged in a lively and enthusiastic discussion. Jenni introduced him, explained why he was there, and indicated a seat at the back of the room where she'd set out for him copies of the handouts she'd be using.

She began by asking Mrs Lambert whether she was still comfortable with where she was sitting, and whether she could see the screen without causing pain to her neck. From the corner of her eye she saw Padraig tapping notes into his tablet. Good. Hopefully that was her first brownie point. In running through the recap of the previous lesson she made sure that she questioned learners by name. The learner she thought of as Newspaper Bob – because he'd refused to put away his newspaper the first time they had met – always had plenty to say these days, so she allowed him plenty of time to show what he knew. She'd found that this was an effective way of keeping him onside. When it came to showing the slides via the data projector, she asked Ponytail Dave if he would make especially clear notes so that Winston, whose arm was still in a sling, could make a copy afterwards. Again, she noticed Padraig busily tap-tapping on his device.

The lesson proceeded entirely to plan. There was, she felt, a friendly and positive working relationship between herself and these adult learners, which her observer could not fail to notice. Even Newspaper Bob kept his interruptions down to a minimum and didn't bang on as long as he sometimes did about issues that were only distantly related to the topic under discussion. In fact, by the time the lesson was drawing to a close and she was conducting a final recap using question and answer, she felt fairly confident that she had done okay.

When the learners had all left the room Padraig came over, smiling, told her he'd enjoyed the lesson, and invited her down to his office so that they could talk about it in detail. As they clattered down the stairs, he asked her how she felt it had gone.

'I thought it went well', she said. 'I mean, it went just as I'd planned it to. And they're such a nice group. They scared me half to death the first time I met them, but now they're lovely.'

'You certainly looked as though you were enjoying teaching them', said Padraig. 'It's great to see that. And some real characters there, eh? Tell me a bit about them.'

So Jenni told him of her first encounter with Newspaper Bob; and about how the seating arrangement had initially caused problems with Mrs Lambert's neck; and how Winston couldn't take notes because of his arm; and how Lucy with the face piercings had objected to the lesson being recorded for his benefit. 'I've explained some of this background in the lesson rationale document', she said.

'You have. You have', said Padraig. 'A great read, if I may say so. Very thorough documentation altogether, Jenni. Well done.'

When they got to his office he offered her the comfy chair and sat across from her smiling. 'Anything else you want to say to me about the lesson before I give you my feedback?'

'I don't think so, no.'

'Okay', said Padraig. 'Well let me say first of all that it was fine. You know it was fine. I was able to tick all the boxes. And I maybe learnt a thing or two myself. There are just a couple of issues I'd like to chat with you about, okay? And hopefully this will be feedback you'll find useful. Because I could just say, yeah, yeah, it was fine – which it was – but then we'd be ignoring this as an opportunity for professional development. So my thinking is: however good we are, there's always something we can learn. Do you agree?'

Jenni nodded. But her smile and her sense of elation was fading fast. She really didn't want to hear about what she could have done better. She just wanted to bask a bit a longer in the fact that it was over and it had gone well.

'So this feller, Bob', said Padraig. 'You had trouble with him at the beginning. And now you feel you've got that sorted, yes?'

Jenni nodded again.

'So how would you describe your strategy there?'

'Well, I think he's a bit resistant to me being in charge', she said. 'Whether it's because I'm younger than him, or I'm a woman, or he doesn't like anyone else to be the boss – I don't know. So I've found that if I let him have the floor a bit, give him plenty of opportunities to say his piece, it seems to keep him happy.'

'And what about the rest them? How would you say they feel about that?'

Jenni wasn't sure how to reply to this. 'Well, I don't know, really', she said. 'I hadn't really thought about it.'

'You see, I did notice one or two of them fidgeting a bit when you let him go on talking for quite a while. And I did see some of them exchanging glances. It was maybe easier for me to see from where I was sitting. But the thing is, Jenni, they may feel he's getting more than his fair share of attention and talking time – which he is – and that's going to annoy them increasingly if it goes on like that. Do you see what's happening there?'

'So my solution to one problem has created another, you mean?'

'I think so. Yes', said Padraig. 'You've sort of solved your issue with him, but now they've got one.'

'So I've got to find a way now of not letting him dominate discussions. Okay. Yes. I'm going to think about that. It might mean selecting teaching and learning methods for a while that avoid opportunities for him to hold forth.'

'Perfect idea!' said Padraig. 'You must let me know if it works. And the only other thing I wanted to discuss with you was the fact that your lesson plan didn't really do the lesson justice. I came in after I read it, expecting I was going to see a rigid, teacher-led lesson with a group of learners going through some very regimented activities – and it wasn't like that at all. Your teaching was responsive and imaginative; the learners were all active and involved, and they were encouraged to use their initiative. It was great. So how are you going to make sure the plan captures all that?'

Jenni, basking in compliments now, smiled. 'I knew that was a problem', she said. 'I just couldn't think how to do it.'

'How about using words and phrases like *respond* and *responsive*; *according to need*; *as appropriate*; *devised by learners*; that sort of thing? And maybe write 'approximately, depending on learners' response/needs' here and there in the timing column. You'll think of some effective ways, I'm sure. Anyway, I'll write up my feedback and get a copy to you by the end of the day. Well done, Jenni.' He held out a hand for her to shake. 'That's one of the most enjoyable lessons I've watched in quite a while.'

Section D

At five o'clock Matt made his way over to Gail Clifford's office for his feedback. He'd managed to rush across town and attend a couple of hours of his teacher training course in the meantime, but he'd found it hard to concentrate on the activities there. His mind kept straying to speculations about what Gail Clifford would have to say about his teaching. His continuing placement depended on her verdict, and so did his future prospects as a teacher. He was pretty confident that the class had gone well, but his earlier experiences with this Assistant Principal had left him still very wary of her.

However, this time the green light was on and her door was slightly ajar. That was a first. So he knocked and walked in.

'Ah! Matt!' Gail Clifford said. She was sitting behind her desk with all his observation documentation spread out in front of her. 'We're going to have to transcribe some of this teacher training documentation into the college format. We use a slightly different lesson plan layout and so on because of inspection requirements. You can get it all off the staff intranet.'

'Happy to do that', said Matt, standing to attention in front of her desk. 'But I don't have access. I'm not a member of staff.'

'Oh', she said. 'Well, then you'll get access when you receive your fractional contract. Sit down. Sit down.' She waved him into a chair.

Fractional contract? He realised he was smiling like an idiot. 'Thank you', he said, and managed somehow to get a serious expression back on his face.

'So on to your feedback', she said briskly. She consulted her notes. 'Right. Well, it was an excellent lesson over all. Clear learning outcomes, learning activities appropriate and engaging. Interactions with learners positive. Learner achievement of outcomes carefully monitored. Nice relaxed teaching style. Good pace.' She glanced up at him. 'I liked the way you handled those awkward questions, by the way. And the fact that you were open with them about your current status. That took some guts. Very professional. So -' she closed the file -'well done. We'll get the contract out to you, soon as. And I'll talk to Finance about payments for cover in the meantime. Nice to have you on board.'

Was that it? thought Matt. Was that all he was going to get by way of feedback? It was very different from the detailed two-way discussion he'd had with Alia following her observation of his teaching. Oh well. He supposed he'd better say something. 'I hope Mo'll be feeling better soon', he said. That sounded suitably gracious and professional, he thought.

'I doubt it', the Assistant Principal said. 'I don't know him well, but I do know he's got chronic health problems. And he's the primary carer for both his aging parents. Life's not easy for him, really.'

Matt didn't know how to respond to that. Instead, emboldened by the positive turn this meeting had taken, he decided he would ask the question he'd been burning to ask for weeks now, which was: What had happened about that envelope of money?

Gail Clifford put her fingertips together and looked at him for a moment or two, frowning. Then she said, 'I'm going to tell you this in confidence, Matt, so it mustn't go any further. Is that clear?'

Matt cleared his throat and nodded.

'I told you – didn't I? – that William bit a student? Well, of course, the student was perfectly well aware that I shouldn't have had him in here on the college premises. No dogs allowed. Apart from guide-dogs, obviously.'

A dog! thought Matt. *She'd been talking about her dog! Of course!*

'I'm not sure why you're smiling', she said sharply.

'Sorry. Sorry. I'm just feeling happy about the contract.'

'Anyway, so he threatened to report it and to sue me personally. I offered to settle it quietly out of court if he'd say no more about it. William was so ill by this time I knew the end was near and I felt I had to keep him with me at all costs. So I paid this nasty man a settlement. It was risky, I know, because he could have come back for more. And then the idiot somehow let the envelope fall out of his bag. Can you believe it? So when you handed it in to me I simply gave it back to him.'

'But what he was doing was blackmail', said Matt, shocked. 'You should go to the police.'

'I don't think I'd have a case', she said. 'Because I offered him the money. I offered to settle. And while I think you're right and his intention was to extort the money from me, I don't think it could be proved. *However*', and she smiled suddenly, 'this character, Colin, since then has shot himself in the foot by urging another student to try the same sort of thing on a member of our staff who inadvertently triggered that student's claustrophobia. And the student has made a formal complaint against Colin, which will almost certainly result in a termination of Colin's enrolment here.'

'Won't he drop you in it before he goes?' asked Matt.

Gail Clifford shrugged her broad shoulders. 'Who cares? What are they going to do? William's gone now. And I can ride out any minor storm in a teacup, believe me.'

Matt believed her.

Jenni was waiting for him, as arranged, in the pub across the road, so that they could tell each other how their observations went. He saw her smiling as he walked in, and that told him everything. He smiled back and gave her the thumbs up. Hurrying across the campus he'd found himself thinking not so much about the contract and his future and the way everything was turning out fine for him, but about how even the most difficult or scary colleagues have their human side, their private sorrows and their vulnerabilities. And the same went for learners. And he knew it was important that he should always try to remember that.

'Come on, then, he said to Jenni, shrugging off his jacket and sitting down heavily on the dusty moquette. 'Tell me what a triumph yours was. And I'll tell you how great mine went. And then – well, I've got such a story to tell you, you won't believe.'

Part two: Critical thinking activities

The following tasks encourage you to think carefully about lesson observations and to reflect on what can be learnt from the experience of having your teaching observed and receiving feedback about it from an experienced colleague, tutor or inspector. They also highlight the importance of both professionalism and empathy in all working interactions.

Activity 1

In this section we learn how Jenni has been preparing for her observation which is to take place that afternoon.

a)   We learn that Jenni had requested to be observed teaching this class soon after she first met them because this was the first time she had taught adults and she felt she needed some feedback and guidance. By the time the observation takes place they have become one of the classes she feels most confident about. What would be your own preference if you were allowed to choose the class you would be observed teaching; one that presented you with difficulties or one that you felt entirely comfortable with? What would be the advantage of this choice? And what might be the potential advantage if you were to choose the other option?

b)   Jenni 'knew that a good lesson plan was essential to a successful observation.' Do you agree? What are the advantages of having a clear, detailed plan of the lesson you are going to be observed teaching?

c)   Jenni is using the college's required format for her lesson plan. We are told that she would have liked an additional column in which to note opportunities for the development of functional or key skills. If you were able to re-design this lesson plan format, what would you change or add, and why?

d)   Jenni is concerned that committing to precise timings in the *Time* column will limit the flexibility she would normally allow herself to extend or adapt activities in response to learners' interest or pace. What is your view on this question? Which do you consider more important: adherence to exact timings or allowance for a degree of flexibility, and why?

e) Jenni is dissatisfied with the *Learner activity* column in her lesson plan. She feels it fails to reflect the variety and learner-centredness of the learning experiences she has planned. What advice would you give her about revising this column of her lesson plan?

f) Jenni clearly finds the *Checklist* from her teacher training days very helpful and reassuring when preparing to be observed. What is your own view of this list? Is there anything you would disagree with? What two additional points of guidance would you suggest adding to this list? Do you have a checklist of your own and if so, how does it compare with Jenni's?

Activity 2

Here we see Matt teaching another of Mo's classes. As well as being thrown into this situation at very short notice with no planning time, he also now discovers, with no warning, that his teaching is to be observed by the Assistant Principal. The following questions allow you to imagine yourself in his situation and to consider, from the safety of your armchair, how you might cope under these circumstances.

a) Matt is not alone in finding Assistant Principal Gail Clifford quite intimidating at the best of times. Now she's sitting at the back of his class, watching him teach, he finds it hard to ignore her presence and carry on as though she wasn't there. How does this compare with your own feelings when your teaching is being observed? How do you cope with having an observer in the classroom? What effect do you think it has on your performance as a teacher? What effect, if any, have you noticed it having on your learners?

b) Luckily, Matt already has an appropriate lesson plan with him from a previous session. This raises an interesting question about the extent to which a lesson should be planned with a specific group of learners in mind. For example, two parallel groups might be more or less identical in terms of ability but might differ drastically in terms of personalities and preferred learning styles. Would you yourself do what Matt does here and use the identical lesson plan, unchanged, for two different classes? Give reasons to support your answer.

c) From observing the learners' body language, Matt is able to tell when they begin to relax and enjoy the lesson. He sees them beginning to smile and uncrossing their arms. What other body language indicators might you observe in a class that was going well? What sorts of body language would tell you that learners were feeling uncomfortable or anxious about the lesson?

d) When Matt invites questions, one learner shouts his question out. How does Matt deal with this? How would you rate his response here? Would you have handled this in the same way and, if not, what would your response have been?

e) Matt knows that it's important to discover and use learners' names. There is evidence here that he doesn't yet know all of them. How can we tell? How does he get around this? Why do you think he uses Britney's name twice?

f) When he is asked whether he'll be replacing Mo, how would you rate his response? Does he deal with this in an effective way? Why is it particularly important in this instance that he is seen to handle the question with care?

g) At the end of the lesson his observer has to rush away, leaving Matt to wait until the end of the afternoon before he gets any feedback. If you were in Matt's place, how would this make you feel? Have you ever had this same experience of having to wait some time before receiving feedback on your teaching? Apart from causing anxiety, what other disadvantages could result from this sort of delay?

Activity 3

In this section Jenni is teaching her class and is being observed by Padraig. A qualified teacher in full-time employment, she nevertheless feels quite nervous about this situation; we learn here about how she copes with this and how she feels about the feedback from her observer.

a) Jenni finds herself in a dilemma over whether to start on time as her observer hasn't arrived by the time the lesson is scheduled to start. What is your view of the way she deals with this? What would you have done in this situation?

b) The topic she discusses with the class while she waits is triggered by a headline relevant to their course. Would you have judged this strategy differently if the headline had not been relevant, and why?

c) Jenni introduces the observer and explains why he's there. Think back to the last time you were observed teaching. Did you introduce the observer? If so, how? Why might this be an important issue?

d) We learn that Jenni indulges Newspaper Bob, letting him dominate the discussion in order to keep him onside. What strategies have you used, if any, to keep the right side of difficult learners? What strategies, if any, do you employ to make sure that no one learner dominates discussions and debates? How important is it, in your view, to ensure that doesn't happen, and why?

e) As soon as the lesson is over, Jenni's observer tells her he enjoyed the lesson. Reflecting on your own experience of being observed, how important is this initial feedback for the teacher's confidence?

f) Before giving her any detailed feedback, Padraig, her observer, asks Jenni how she herself feels the lesson went. Why do you think he does this? Is this a question you yourself have been asked following an observation? How easy do you find it to reflect on the success or otherwise of a lesson immediately afterwards? How would you describe the difference between an evaluation made to an observer and one that you write up for yourself – for example, in a reflective journal? From a professional point of view, which would you consider the most useful, and why?

g) Before giving his detailed feedback, Padraig asks Jenni to tell him a little about the learners. Why do you think he does this?

h) What is your view of Padraig's argument that an observed lesson, however excellent, should be used as a learning opportunity for the teacher? This is his justification for pointing out a couple of developmental points for Jenni. If you were in Jenni's place, how useful would you find this part of his feedback?

i) He makes some suggestions about how Jenni might edit the *Learner activity* column of her lesson plan. How do these compare with the revisions you advised in Activity 1?

Activity 4

Matt receives positive observation feedback and some good news from Gail Clifford. He also finally unravels the mystery of the money in the envelope that he found on his first day at the college. This meeting acts as an important reminder to him that everyone has their problems and their vulnerabilities, and that the behaviour of difficult colleagues – just like that of difficult learners – may well arise from problems and anxieties of which he knows nothing.

a) Look again at how Gail Clifford begins her feedback to Matt. How would you rate this as a way of opening their meeting, and why?

b) What indication is there at the beginning of their meeting that both Matt and the Assistant Principal are interacting in a way that emphasises their difference in rank rather than their shared interest as colleagues?

c) Compare the manner and content of Gail Clifford's feedback with that given by Padraig to Jenni in section C. Reflecting on your own experience of receiving feedback on your teaching, which of these two approaches would you find most helpful, and why?

d) The Assistant Principal here divulges information to Matt about a colleague, Mo's, personal circumstances. In your view, is she behaving here within the parameters of acceptable professional behaviour? Are there circumstances in which she would be justified in disclosing this information? Is this situation one of them?

e) Why is it important, as Matt reminds himself, to keep in mind that colleagues and learners may have problems of which we are not aware?

f) What do you think the *story* is that Matt is promising to tell Jenni? Of everything that was said in his meeting with Gail Clifford, what would he be justified in disclosing now, and what should he keep to himself out of professional discretion?

And finally...

» *You will find some helpful texts relating to observations and how to prepare for them listed under Further Reading at the back of this book.*

» *What happens next? That will depend on you!*

Further reading

The following suggestions for further reading are intended to help you to follow up and find out more about the topics and issues addressed in each story. You'll find that some publications are listed under more than one chapter. There are two reasons for this. One is that the range of issues encountered on a typical working day in a Further Education college are not easily compartmentalised. A key topic in the first story, for example, is lesson planning; but this is not the only issue that concerns the teacher on that particular day. The other reason for some texts popping up more than once is that they are books that cover many aspects of working in FE, from planning and assessing to the theories and principles of learning that underpin good practice.

Because one of the key aims of this book is to encourage reflection and reflective practice – and because this is a theme that runs across and between all the stories – you may find it useful to explore this aspect of professional practice further. You will find chapters on reflective practice in some of the texts recommended as further reading for the stories. But the following three texts deal exclusively with the topic, and will point you to other important sources of information about key theories and practices.

Appleyard, N and Appleyard, K (2015) *Reflective Teaching and Learning in Further Education*. Northwich: Critical Publishing.

Roffey-Barentsen, J and Malthouse, R (2013) *Reflective Practice in Education and Training*. London: Sage/Learning Matters.

Rushton, I and Suter, M (2012) *Reflective Practice for Teaching in Lifelong Learning*. Maidenhead: Open University Press.

Story 1: The best laid plans: planning a lesson

Curzon, L B and Tummons, J (2013) *Teaching in Further Education*. London: Bloomsbury.

Gravells, J and Wallace, S (2013) *The A-Z Guide to Working in Further Education*. Northwich: Critical Publishing.

Rossa, J (2014) *The Perfect Further Education Lesson*. London: Independent Thinking Press (Crown House Publishing).

Wallace, S (2011) *Teaching, Tutoring and Training in the Lifelong Learning Sector* (4th Edition). Exeter: Learning Matters.

Story 2: Assessing learner needs and assessing learning

Armitage, A and Renwick, M (2008) *Assessment in FE: A practical guide for lecturers*. London: Continuum.

Gravells, A (2011) *Principles and Practice of Assessment in the Lifelong Learning Sector (Further Education and Skills)*. Exeter: Learning Matters.

Tummons, J (2011) *Assessing Learning in the Lifelong Learning Sector* (Achieving QTLS Series) (3rd Edition). Exeter: Learning Matters.

Wallace, S (2011) *Teaching, Tutoring and Training in the Lifelong Learning Sector* (4th Edition). Exeter: Learning Matters.

Story 3: Selecting methods and strategies

Curzon, L B and Tummons, J (2013) *Teaching in Further Education*. London: Bloomsbury.

Duckworth, V (2013) *How to Be a Brilliant FE Teacher: A Practical Guide to Being Effective and Innovative*. London: Routledge.

Wallace, S (2011) *Teaching, Tutoring and Training in the Lifelong Learning Sector* (4th Edition). Exeter: Learning Matters.

Story 4: Motivating learners and encouraging appropriate behaviour

Vizard, D (2012) *How to Manage Behaviour in Further Education*. London: Sage.

Wallace, S (2007) *Getting the Buggers Motivated in FE*. London: Continuum/Bloomsbury.

Wallace, S (2013) *Managing Behaviour in Further and Adult Education*. London: Sage/Learning Matters.

Story 5: Inclusion, equality and diversity

Peart, S (2014) *Equality and Diversity in Further Education*. Northwich: Critical Publishing.

Peart, S (2013) *Making Education Work: How Black Men and Boys Navigate the Further Education Sector*. London: IoE Press.

Spenceley, L (2014) *Inclusion in Further Education*. Northwich: Critical Publishing.

Story 6: Working with adult learners

Dweck, C (2012) *Mindset: How You Can Fulfil Your Potential*. London: Robinson.

Rogers, A and Horrocks, N (2010) *Teaching Adults*. Maidenhead: Open University Press.

Rogers, J (2007) *Adults Learning*. Maidenhead: Open University Press.

Scruton, J and Ferguson, B (2014) *Teaching and Supporting Adult Learners*. Northwich: Critical Publishing.

Wallace, S (2013) *Managing Behaviour in Further and Adult Education*. London: Sage/Learning Matters.

Story 7: Being a subject specialist

Appleyard, K and Appleyard, N (2014) *The Professional Teacher in Further Education*. Northwich: Critical Publishing.

Wallace, S (2011) *Teaching, Tutoring and Training in the Lifelong Learning Sector* (4th Edition). Exeter: Learning Matters.

Story 8: Making the most of mentoring

Gravells, J and Wallace, S (2012) *Dial M for Mentor*. Northwich: Critical Publishing.

Gravells, J and Wallace, S (2007) *Mentoring in the Further Education Sector*. Exeter: Learning Matters.

Story 9: Good professional: good colleague

Appleyard, K and Appleyard, N (2014) *The Professional Teacher in Further Education*. Northwich: Critical Publishing.

Wallace, S (2013) *Understanding the Further Education Sector*. Northwich: Critical Publishing.

Story 10: Showing what you can do: performing well in lesson observations

Wallace, I and Kirkman, L (2014) *Pimp Your Lesson!: Prepare, Innovate, Motivate and Perfect* (3rd Edition). London: Bloomsbury.

Wallace, S (2011) *Teaching, Tutoring and Training in the Lifelong Learning Sector* (4th Edition). Exeter: Learning Matters.

Index